CBS SPORTS PRESENTS

STORIES FROM THE FINAL FOUR.

Edited by Matt Fulks

Foreword by Jim Nantz

CBS Sports presents : stories from the final four / edited by Matt Fulks ; foreword by
Jim Nantz.
    p.cm.
    ISBN 1-886110-97-2 (pbk.)
    1. NCAA Basketball Tournament—History.2. NCAA Basketball
    Tournament—Anecdotes. I. Fulks, Matt. II. CBS Sports.

    GV885.49.N37 C28 2000
    796.323'63'0973—dc21   99-089751

Dedication

To my wife, Libby, with whom
(to paraphrase the movie *Fletch*)
I have my own version of one-on-one.
Without you, this book isn't possible.

TABLE OF CONTENTS

Part IV: The '80s

Part V: The '90s

Acknowledgments

Considering this book was assembled with the swiftness of Michael Jordan's cross-over step (hopefully, reading it, you won't realize that), a ton of people need to be thanked for their involvement. As always, too many people. Since I'm over my word-count, and now have to start paying about 23-cents a word, you may not be mentioned by name. Don't take it personally ... I'm sure I was thinking of you. Thanks to the following, who offered game ideas, contact help, and/or support: Pat Bennett, Tim Brando, Wes Durham, Brian Estridge, Gary Gupton, Matt Kalman, Don Meyer, Dale Ratermann, Bil Ryckman, Ken Samelson, Shannon Terry, Fred White. Special thanks to John Feinstein who offered a good laugh and encouragement on D-Day.

To the Sports Information Directors and their staffs, plus the various Men's Basketball Administrative Assistants, who are probably tired of me, for providing media guides, contacts, various stories for the book, and contact with a few of the coaches. The most helpful were: Hanna Broda, Dean Buchan, Judy Cowgill, Mike Cragg, Jeff Darby, Gary Johnson at the NCAA, Steve Kirschner, Tony Neely, Joan Owens, Rick Poulter, Mike Sheridan, Doug Vance and Amy Wamester.

In addition to various newspaper articles and media guides, a forest-full of books was used as research material for this book, and to clutter my desk. The main ones have been: *Inside Sports Magazine's College Basketball Guide* by Mike Douchant; the *1999 ESPN Information Please Sports Almanac*; *Against All Odds* by Chuck Woodling; *Hoopla* by Peter C. Bjarkman; *Max and the Jayhawks* by Max Falkenstien and Doug Vance; *Giant Steps* by Kareem Abdul-Jabbar and Peter Knobler; *The Sportscaster's Dozen* by Matt Fulks; *They Call Me Coach* by John Wooden with Jack Tobin; *Hoop Hysteria* — Volumes I and II by Brent Flanders, Jeff Sigler, Randy Towner and Doug Vance; *A Coach's Life* by Dean Smith; *The Greatest Book of College Basketball* by Blair Kerkhoff; and *100 Greatest Basketball Moments of All Time* by Alex Sachare

To each of the athletes and coaches, broadcasters and writers, who contributed stories. Your stories are amazing ... hopefully as good in print as in person. Obviously this project, and some of our greatest basketball memories, are not possible without you.

Thank you to Jim Nantz, one of the most down-to-earth people in this business, for your willingness to write a great foreword and offer words of advice. Special thanks to legendary UCLA coach John Wooden. It was an extreme honor and joy to talk to you so often during this project. To my main outside editor, Joe Lofaro, who has been reminded why he got out of the business of editing. To John Hadley and Brad Winters. To Keith Ritter, Terry Ewert, Eric Mann and Eileen Bramswig at CBS Sports, for your time and encouragement. To An Beard, Bob Snodgrass and the rest of Addax Publishing, for keeping me on a straight course, and helping this become "our" project. Also, to Trey, Tom and Brian at Hakan & Associates, CBS Sports' Exclusive Licensing Agency. Special thanks to Melissa Caito, Dennis Cryder and Tom Jernstedt with the NCAA as well as Eric Barnhart, Marc Kidd and Jim Host of Host Communications.

To Barry Landes; Don McLaughlin; John and Alicia Wood; MoJo and Jelaine; PKing; Gig; Tom Lawrence; Wiss; Kevin and Sarah Oats; my in-laws, Todd and Pat Burwell; my parents, Fred and Sharon; my brother Josh; my daughter, Helen, who has been subjected to more Veggie Tales and Teletubby videos the past few weeks than any one child needs to be; and my best friend, Libby, who puts up with my writing quirks and Elvis habits ... you've got your husband again.

Introduction

Each March, college basketball captures the heart of (seemingly) every person for three weekends. Synonymous with that period known as "March Madness," is the network that has brought the games home to Americans since 1982 ... CBS.

Other networks have carried the NCAA Tournament, but none has single-handedly taken the tournament to a higher level because of that coverage. During each tournament, CBS brings out the emotion that is fostered when a group of 18-22 year old student-athletes battle for one common goal ... the national championship.

Since 1982, some of the greatest or best known names in basketball have relished in the opportunity to play in college basketball's most heralded two-game event. Michael Jordan. Patrick Ewing. James Worthy. Hakeem Olajuwon. Clyde Drexler. Danny Manning. Christian Laettner. Grant Hill.

But this book goes further back, to a time when CBS didn't own the rights, to a time when the idea of nationally televised games was as much of a dream as flying to the moon. Look where we are today. In 1999, manned space shuttle launches are nearly commonplace, and CBS paid $6 billion for exclusive rights through 2013 for not only television coverage of the NCAA Tournament, but also radio, cable television; satellite, digital and home video; and the Internet.

The names of players involved in the Final Four from 1952 until 1981 are also tied with the tag of greatness. Clyde Lovellette. Wilt Chamberlain. Lew Alcindor (Kareem Abdul-Jabbar). Bill Walton. Kent Benson. Larry Bird. Magic Johnson. Gregory Kelser. Darrell Griffith.

When the idea of *CBS Sports Presents: Stories from the Final Four* was first discussed with me, it seemed like a no-brainer. For a college basketball fan to be able to collect stories from some of the greatest players and coaches (of course, broadcasters and writers, too) ever to walk on the hardwood, and put it in a book was a dream come true. Someone once said that "we do things in dreams that we would normally not dream of doing." I could never have imagined, or dreamed, of working with these legends in this type of project.

Almost immediately, however, the question became, how does one go about picking the games featured in a book such as this? For me, it was a matter of taking the easy way out ... getting other people involved. A group of 10 college basketball announcers and die-hard fans were asked to pick their top 10 games throughout the history of the Final Four.

Some of the games featured in *Stories from the Final Four* are assumed, such as the 1968 UCLA-Houston semifinal; the 1979 Michigan State-Indiana State game; the 1983 North Carolina State championship; Villanova against Georgetown in 1985; and the 1992 Duke Blue Devils team. Those games were picked by the majority of the voters.

Other games may have been selected for their historical significance such as the 1952 championship game, which was the first year that four teams played in the same location in a "Final Four" type format; or the 1966 championship which, today, has been seen as the game that broke down color barriers when an all-black starting five for Texas Western defeated an all-white Kentucky team.

There will probably be some debates on a couple of the games included, or not included, but that's fine. This list of 21 games undoubtedly contains some of the best moments in the history of the Final Four.

Once we had decided on the games, the task was to come up with the best possible story contributors. I can truly say without equivocation that each of the storytellers in this book were on our original wish list. Three people turned us down because of other book and/or time commitments. Since this group was hand-picked, it is safe to say that we could not have picked better, more humble, men for this book. For me to begin singling out my favorites would be a waste of time because every single storyteller's name included in this book would be mentioned as a favorite.

You may notice that there are no photographs. What, no pictures in a sports book? As you read through this collection of stories, you will notice that no photographs were needed. The impeccable memories of these storytellers are incredible ... but then again, for most, going to the Final Four is not a memory that is easily forgotten. Imagine ...

M.W.F.
1/00

Foreword
by Jim Nantz

———

March Madness and The Road to the Final Four has been part of CBS' Sports since 1982. We have a multitude of memories and certainly more than "One Shining Moment."

Prior to my days at CBS, I had first experienced the Final Four in 1981 courtesy of Guy Lewis, the University of Houston's legendary basketball coach. Lewis had given me, a college senior at the time, my start in television as the host of his weekly program. We went to Philadelphia that year to tape his final show of the season with hopes of returning to the Final Four the following year with his team in tow. Sure enough, the next year, the burgeoning Phi Slamma Jamma Cougars made the first of three consecutive trips to college basketball's Promised Land.

In 1983, my alma mater was set to provide me with the ultimate Final Four memory: a national championship. A year earlier I had left the Houston market for a television position at the CBS affiliate in Salt Lake City. I was scheduled to anchor the sports on Monday night, April the 4th, the night my Cougars were set for their coronation against North Carolina State. Thankfully, my boss understood the gravity of the occasion and allowed me to fly to Albuquerque for the final.

I rode to "The Pit" on the Houston team bus, sliding my 6'3" body into the arena by hiding amongst the far more impressive frames of Olajuwon, Drexler, Micheaux and Young. Once clear of security, I was free to squeeze into any open space. I found the perfect location near the Houston bench that was even all the more alluring due to its location next to Brent Musburger's broadcast position. From my seat, I could almost reach out and touch the CBS icon. I spent most of the championship game with my head on a swivel - watching the action on the court occasionally, but devoting most of my time to inspecting Brent's every move. He was the coolest, smoothest anchor I had ever seen. Lost in admiration, I fantasized what it must be like to host America's greatest sports spectacle. Three years later, I was sitting in his chair.

My Cougars were denied a national championship that night in New Mexico. Lorenzo Charles dunked our title dreams away. I must have stood there for a solid hour in disbelief before it was time to ride back on the bus to the team hotel.

To this day, the sting of that loss still lingers. Yet, that Final Four remains special to me. It was inside "The Pit" where I was exposed to CBS Sports up close for the first time. Although the network didn't know me, I vowed that someday our paths would cross again. Somehow, by being in the presence of Brent, I had been inspired and at the same time reassured that my lifelong quest to work for CBS Sports was now attainable.

One of the greatest honors of my life has been helping CBS Sports navigate the road to the Final Four every March. Since 1986, I have formed warm and treasured memories from the absurd of the dunking exhibition by Andre "The Creator" Wiley of Oklahoma, who jumped over folding chairs during the Friday practice of the 1988 Final Four, to the poignancy of seeing John Wooden on hand in Seattle in 1995 to see the UCLA Bruins win their first championship since he had retired.

The one moment I never let go of comes each year at the end of the broadcast. Along with my esteemed partner and wonderful friend, Billy Packer, I stand at midcourt, absorbing the wide range of emotions. We sign off with our annual CBS anthem, "One Shining Moment." As the poignant piece rolls to millions across America, it also plays throughout the building on a giant screen. I observe players, coaches, spectators, and even hardened media members, pausing in unison to the closing video montage of a magical month. I look into the stands to see both tri-umphant and defeated fans misty-eyed. Whether they are shedding tears of joy or tears of sorrow, all of them feel blessed to have been a part of the experience. I know, I've been there. They have formed a memory they will cherish the rest of their lives. For me, I look around the arena and think back to 1983 when my championship dreams were defeated, yet where my career dreams were crystallized. There is nothing quite like the Final Four and I am so thankful to be a part of it.

In *CBS Sports Presents: Stories from the Final Four*, you're going to be reading similar memories from a fascinating variety of perspectives from coaches and players to some of my colleagues in the media, each memory deeply personal and unique to that individual. I am sure you will enjoy reliving these experiences and remembering some of your own.

Part I: The '50s

CHAPTER 1

Seattle, Washington
March 25-26, 1952

The 1952 season featured a landmark change in the NCAA Tournament with the addition of a national semifinal, known today as the Final Four. Through the 1951 national tournament, four regional finalists would play each other in two different sites with the two winners advancing to the national championship game. In 1952, that round of regional finalists became known as the national semifinal with the four teams playing in the same location.

The Kansas Jayhawks, under the direction of head coach "Phog" Allen, reached the championship game against Frank McGuire's St. John's team after losing only three games during the season. On the court, the Jayhawks were led by center Clyde Lovellette, who led the nation with a 28.4 points per game scoring average. Lovellette is the only player in NCAA history to lead the nation in scoring the same year his team won the national championship. He also averaged 13.2 rebounds a game during his senior season.

In the championship game between St. John's and Kansas, which the Jayhawks won 80-63, Lovellette led all scorers with 33 points. Because of his play throughout the NCAA Tournament, Lovellette was named the Most Outstanding Player of the Tournament.

After graduating from Kansas, Lovellette played in the National

Basketball Association for Minneapolis, Cincinnati, St. Louis and Boston. He was elected to the Naismith Basketball Hall of Fame in 1988. Today, Clyde Lovellette is enjoying the retired life in his home state of Indiana.

1952 All-Tournament Team
James Bredar, Illinois
Dean Kelley, Kansas
John Kerr, Illinois
Clyde Lovellette, Kansas
  (Most Outstanding Player)
Ron MacGllvray, St. John's
Bob Zawoluk, St. John's

Final Four Participants
Illinois
Kansas
St. John's
Santa Clara

National Semifinals
St. John's 61, Illinois 59
Kansas 74, Santa Clara 55

National Championship
Kansas 80, St. John's 63

Clyde Lovellette

The thing that sticks in my mind the most when I think back to our championship season of 1952 is that when I was being recruited in high school by Kansas head coach Dr. Forrest "Phog" Allen, he told me that with the other recruits he was bringing in, if we stayed together and played as a unit, we would have a chance to win the national championship and an Olympic gold medal. He told me that the only other ingredient he needed to fill the team was a big guy in the middle. That was complimentary to think he felt I could be a key player in his scheme of the basketball program.

Before that time, I had not heard anything about the Kansas program or Coach Allen. In this part of the Midwest, Indiana, we didn't get any type of news about Kansas. The only news we heard was about our local schools such as Indiana University, Purdue, Notre Dame and Indiana State. Every kid in our area was going to one of those schools. For that reason, I knew little about Kansas, their tradition and Phog, even though he was one of the greatest coaches in the college ranks. So, when I heard that Phog Allen and Kansas was recruiting me, that didn't mean a lot until I met him, talked to him and heard his plan. Before that point, I was headed to Indiana University, which is where everybody around here expected me to go. All of my coaches were from IU, so that was the only program I heard about, and it was the one program I saw first-hand. When Phog came calling, my college future became a completely different picture.

Going to the state of Kansas, visiting the campus, seeing Hoch Auditorium, hearing about the Kansas basketball tradition and Phog Allen the man, and realizing that he was coached by the James Naismith, the father of the game, my decision was made. Growing up I didn't know much about the history of the game, and didn't particularly care who invented it, but once I visited Kansas and the realization hit that here's a man who was coached by the man who invented the game of basketball ... my goodness. You have to stop and marvel at that fact.

Phog Allen had accomplished a number of things through the years: coaching three teams at one time in a season or putting on the gear at 60-plus years of age to show players different moves. Phog turned out great coaches, too, like Adolph Rupp, Dean Smith and Ralph Miller, among others.

Allen was a marvel and a great psychologist. He could get players to cry, or make us mad, or any other feeling imaginable. If the team wasn't playing well and he wanted to make us mad, he knew what buttons to push. He could show a picture to us or read a story to us to get a certain emotion aroused before we went out on the floor. All of that was wrapped up in this man that I really admired. The more I got to know him, the more I realized what kind of a great man was coaching me, not only in basketball but in life as well.

In Lawrence, Kan., I found a great area in which to play out my college basketball career. The other kids that Allen had recruited in my class, such as Bill Lienhard, Bill Hougland, John Keller and Bob Kenney, were a great bunch of guys, almost like brothers.

Like most family situations, times on the court weren't always great. Because of NCAA regulations at the time, we were not eligible to play for the varsity during our freshman year. Our sophomore and junior seasons were iffy at best, only reaching the NCAA Tournament's first round on one occasion. Our senior year was the pinnacle. Going into our senior season, we realized that we only had one more season to make Phog's dream come true of our group winning the national title and going to the Olympics. That was in the back of our minds throughout that season.

We never really considered reaching Phog's goal as a reason for pressure, but there was a reality that we could accomplish what we had set out to accomplish. The team only had one more shot, because it was our senior year, plus it was an Olympic year. We had to stay focused on what we were doing and literally took things game-by-game. Each game was played as if it were the last one, thinking that we had to win that game to play again. Over the course of the season, we lost back-to-back games at the end of January to Kansas State and Oklahoma State, both on the road. From that point on, the team had to regroup, thinking that we couldn't lose like that again. Then we had the good strength to keep winning throughout the rest of the season and the tournament. After each game we knew we were getting closer and closer to the goal that Phog had set. Finally, it was reality, this team had come full circle ... we were going to play for the national championship.

No matter who came on the court with us during that 1952 tournament, we easily won. Even during stages of individual games when things would get close, our momentum would pick us up and help us win. We were on a roll. Our closest game in the tournament was the opening contest with Texas Christian, escaping with a 68-64 victory.

St. John's, our opponent in the finals, had a good team with guys such as Ron MacGilvray and Bob Zawoluk. They were also playing well, having knocked off the top-ranked Kentucky Wildcats in the East Regionals, ending Kentucky's 23-game winning streak. Neither us nor the Redmen were touted to be in the finals.

The title game was one in which our team could do no wrong; everything seemed to come together for us that night against St. John's. It really wasn't much of a game, and the final score of 80-63 would indicate that. During the early part of the game it was close, but after awhile we started to dominate them.

The closest call of the tournament for me was between our two Final Four games. The Final Four was played in Seattle, Wash., that season. One of my fraternity brothers was working on a Coast Guard cruiser, and he took me out in Puget Sound. We got stuck in the fog and couldn't get back to shore. I happened to get into the hotel quite late, or actually, early on the morning of the championship game.

There was a newspaper reporter in the lobby of the hotel when I returned. He looked up, saw me, and looked back down at his paper. The story never broke in the paper. I had quite a fear of not being allowed to play against St. John's, because not only had I missed curfew, but I got back extremely late. To this day I don't even know if Phog ever knew about that incident. Evidently I got enough rest, considering I went out and played a pretty good ballgame against St. John's.

I was fortunate to lead all scorers with 33 points that night. A lot of the credit needs to go to my teammates. If it weren't for the specific players we had getting the ball to me, I wouldn't have been as successful. These guys were completely unselfish; they could have frozen me out if they wanted, but they didn't. It goes along with the idea of thinking we were a family and we knew our roles. Kenney had a role, Lienhard had a role, and so on. My role was on the scoring and rebounding end. I wouldn't have cared if Kenney got 40 points and I didn't get any, because we wanted to win for Kansas, for Phog and for ourselves. We just jelled that season.

The other members of our team knew that I could score inside the paint and surrounding the lane, plus they knew that nobody we played against could stop me down low. The only time that teams posed a threat was when they double-teamed or triple-teamed me inside. As an individual, one-on-one, there was no player who could stop me, or at least I can't remember any player in particular who gave me fits. I had my bad games, but it wasn't necessarily the defensive player who held me; it was more of my inability to put the ball in the hole. The other guys on our team picked up on that and, on my good nights, worked to get the ball inside.

That was the way things went the entire season. Because of their assists that whole year, I led the nation in scoring with 795 points, becoming the only player in NCAA history to lead the country in scoring the same year his team won the national title. Even though all records are made to be broken sooner or later, surprisingly, that one has stood the test of time.

The main reason that record has lasted is because there aren't a lot of scorers playing for the main NCAA Division-I schools. The big scorers are with the smaller schools that may not get a chance to play in the NCAA Tournament. The guy who has come the closest to equaling the feat is Glenn Robinson of Purdue in the 1993-1994 season. He led the nation in scoring with 1,030 points and was the National Player of the Year. Purdue was knocked off by Duke in the Southeast Regional Finals. Robinson would have done it if Purdue had kept winning. That was the biggest scare that I've had with that record.

That 1952 season was truly unique for our team.

Once we had won the national championship, we had one more goal to reach for Coach Allen – the Olympics. After beating St. John's, we had to play the champion of the NIT, La Salle, with the great Tom Gola, in New York's Madison Square Garden for the college championship. An AAU team from Peoria, Ill., played Phillips Petroleum for the Industrial League Championship. Peoria beat Phillips and we beat La Salle, setting up a meeting between the AAU team and us to determine the head coach of the Olympic squad.

Peoria led much of the game, until we were able to forge a tremendous comeback in the second half. In the last minute of the ballgame, with a tied score, I stole the ball from Mark Freiberger, and drove down the court with Jayhawks on each side of me. All I had to do was give one of them the ball for an easy layup and a two-point lead. For whatever reason, I tried to take the ball the whole way, mistimed my jump and blew the shot. Howie Williams from Peoria got the ball off the outlet pass, launched a shot from midcourt, it went in and they beat us by two points. That win made their coach, Warren Womble, the Olympic team's

In 1952, Clyde Lovellette of Kansas became the first player to lead the nation in scoring the same season his team won the national championship.

head coach and Phog the assistant. Had we won that game Phog would have been the head coach.

We had that chance within reach, but for some reason I felt that I could be the hero. I don't know what, if anything, was going through my mind. I had a clear shot at that basket with no opponents around and two Kansas guys next to me, but I blew it.

Those kinds of plays really stick in a player's mind. It was just a game, and we were going to the Olympics anyway, but winning would have been a beautiful topping on Phog's cake. Unfortunately we didn't win.

Seven guys from the Kansas team went to the 1952 Olympics in Helsinki, five from Peoria and two from Phillips. Going to the Olympics was special, especially since half of us were still in college. There is so much professionalism in amateur athletics today that the athletes almost aren't true amateurs anymore. It means a lot to the NBA players who now represent the United States, but I think it meant a little more to us.

Regardless, we won the gold medal and Phog was still with us so I guess it wasn't that bad. It's amazing to think that the gold medal represents the United States. I always felt that I was playing first for the United States of America, second for Kansas and third for Lovellette. The national championship was for the University of Kansas, the state of Kansas, for Phog and then myself. It was such a great honor to represent the United States, that winning the gold medal would have to be a little above the NCAA title.

To represent a country rather than a state is something special, but to be able to win the Olympic gold medal with six college teammates from that NCAA team, is truly exceptional. At Kansas we were like a family going through our four years of school. I don't think there's a ballplayer Phog had on the court that didn't love him and wouldn't go through the walls for him. That's the kind of coach for whom I played.

Stories From the Final Four: The '50s

There are probably people out there who know more about Phog Allen than I do, but if they try to talk negatively to me about him, I won't listen. All of the things that I know about Phog are positive, and those are the memories I want to keep with me. None of us is perfect, and we all have our quirks, but as far as I was concerned, if there could be a perfect man at that time, he was the one.

There were some ups and downs, then in 1952 everything came together, including Phog's predictions. A plan couldn't have been drawn up any better than the way Phog Allen drew up ours.

CHAPTER 2

Kansas City, Missouri
March 22-23, 1957

Like a few other seasons throughout the history of the NCAA Tournament, the 1957 championship game featured a seemingly unbeatable team, Kansas, against the undefeated North Carolina Tar Heels. The Jayhawks were heavy favorites largely because of their dominating sophomore center, Wilt Chamberlain.

As North Carolina's leading scorer that season, Lennie Rosenbluth, says, "It might be the only time in history that the undefeated number-one team in the nation went into the championship game as the underdog." He may be right. Some betting lines had Kansas close to a double-digit favorite.

Rosenbluth was one player that concerned most teams throughout that undefeated season for the Tar Heels. He was one of the leading scorers in the nation with his 28.0 average per game (Chamberlain averaged 29.6). After graduating from Carolina, Rosenbluth enjoyed a short career of professional basketball before becoming a history teacher in the Miami area. He still lives in Miami.

Jerry Waugh was an assistant coach for first-year Kansas head coach Dick Harp. Legendary head coach Phog Allen reached the mandatory retirement age for Kansas, and had to step down. Harp caught some unfair flack in his new position. Waugh joined the Jayhawks at the perfect time ... Chamberlain's first season on the varsity team in a year the team reached the NCAA title game. Waugh was one of Harp's assistant coaches until 1960.

The name Max Falkenstien has been synonymous with the University of Kansas athletics for more than 50 years as one of the few radio voices for the Jayhawks. In 1957 he co-hosted a radio show with Chamberlain called *Flippin' with the Dipper*. The show was short-lived as Jayhawk head coach Dick Harp was concerned about possible NCAA infractions. Although Chamberlain was not paid to do the show, there were paid sponsors.

After playing a triple-overtime game against Michigan State in the semifinals, the Tar Heels outlasted the Jayhawks in another triple-overtime, 54-53.

1957 All-Tournament Team	Final Four Participants
Pete Brennan, North Carolina	Kansas
Gene Brown, San Francisco	Michigan State
Wilt Chamberlain, Kansas	North Carolina
(Most Outstanding Player)	San Francisco
John Green, Michigan State	
Lennie Rosenbluth, North Carolina	

National Semifinals	National Championship
North Carolina 74,	UNC 54, Kansas 53 (3 OT)
Michigan State 70 (3 OT)	
Kansas 80, San Francisco 56	

Max Falkenstien

The 1957 season was one in which the Kansas Jayhawks would have been considered a failure if they did not win the national championship. That season, Wilt Chamberlain arrived on the scene as the most widely recruited high school player in the history of the game and Dick Harp took over as head coach after the legendary Phog Allen had been forced into retirement. After Dr. Allen left coaching against his wishes, he said, "Anybody could win the national championship with Wilt Chamberlain and four cheerleaders." Needless to say, that put a lot of pressure on the new coach.

Truly, Wilt was an amazing athlete but that kind of burden on Dick and him, coupled with the fact that Harp was replacing a legend, was probably unfair. Wilt was able to do things on and off the basketball court that amazed people. His prowess in track and field was magnificent, such as throwing the shot with people like Olympic medalists Bill Nieder and Al Oerter; winning the Big Eight High Jump title at 6-6 3/4 with no practice; finishing second in the Kansas Relays; lifting weights with one hand that Nieder and Oerter were struggling to lift with two. Those kinds of phenomenal stories of his strength are what set Wilt on a different plateau than most other athletes.

During his varsity debut that season, on December 3, against Northwestern, Wilt scored 52 points, a Jayhawk single-game scoring record, and pulled down an amazing 31 rebounds. His career-high 52 points remains the only single-game scoring record in a varsity debut in the NCAA.

I have had a very close relationship with almost all of the athletes here at Kansas, but Wilt had a bit of a shield around him. I couldn't say that he and I were friends, we were acquaintances. Wilt was just a little bit different than almost any other player who has come to KU. He wasn't the typical college student. He didn't socialize a lot with his classmates; instead, he would go to Kansas City and Topeka to see friends who weren't necessarily college people.

Our closest relationship was the fact that we had a radio program together on WREN in Topeka. A few years before Wilt, in 1952, I had a radio program with Clyde Lovellette when he was playing for the Jayhawks. He had a mythical buddy, his hound dog, Lester. He liked country music, so our program was built around that. Wilt's choice of music was entirely different than Clyde's. Chamberlain's show was called *Flippin' with the Dipper*. He'd bring some tunes to the station, and we'd talk some basketball ... we had a good time. The program lasted about eight weeks because Harp started to get nervous about it being an NCAA violation. (We didn't pay Wilt anything for doing the program, but there were commercials on the show.)

That was about the extent of my relationship with Wilt, except for the time he took my car for a ride. I had a tiny Renault 4CV3 car. The thing was so small, it could barely be considered a car ... it wasn't much larger than a golf cart. One day Wilt said to me, "I'd sure like to take a little spin in that car." I told him to go ahead and drive it around the fieldhouse. When he got in the car, his knees practically hit the ceiling. I'll never forget the sight. When he came back from his test drive he said, "I think this is too small for me."

Off the court, Wilt almost single-handedly stopped segregation in this part of Kansas. When he first came to Lawrence, the restaurants were all segregated. In the theaters, the blacks had to sit in the balcony or in the back rows. Wilt, with his awesome presence, helped change all of that. A popular student hang-out in Lawrence was the Dine-A-Mite on 23rd Street, where Roy and Mary Borgen (two great KU basketball fans) were the proprietors. One day Wilt went in there, headed to one of the booths and sat down. Roy and Mary came over, asked him what he wanted and served him. From that moment on, the color line was sort of broken in Lawrence.

He made a lot of changes in Lawrence, Kan., and throughout the Midwest just because he was such a dominant and powerful individual.

Coaching Wilt was not a simple situation for Harp. Many Kansas people who recruited Wilt had led him to believe that Phog Allen would be his coach, but that was not to be the case. Doc reached the mandatory retirement age of 70, and the Kansas Board of Regents refused to make an exception that would have allowed him to continue coaching.

The team went through the 1956-1957 season very successfully, not recording its first loss of the year until its 13th game, against Iowa State in Ames, 39-37. The Cyclones played a box-and-one that game, with the box around Chamberlain. The other Iowa State player chased whoever had the ball for Kansas. That was the first indication in college that Wilt was not going to be able to do the things he skillfully could do. He began to have a negative feeling about college basketball from that point forward.

The Jayhawks finished the regular season with a 21-2 record and headed to Dallas for the Midwest Region of the NCAA Tournament. Unfortunately, not all of the Jayhawks were welcomed by everyone in Texas. Maurice King, one of the first black players at Kansas, was in his third year when Wilt arrived on the scene. Because the Kansas team featured two black players, there were a lot of racial problems on the Dallas trip.

When the Jayhawks got to Dallas for the tournament, the hotel to which the team had been assigned would not accept any black guests. Harp decided, "If we can't all stay together, none of us will be staying here. We're not going to put Maurice and Wilt in private homes." So the

 Solly Walker of St. John's became the first black player on the court at Kentucky's Memorial Coliseum. He played sparingly in that December 17, 1951 game.

whole team stayed in Grand Prairie, Texas, a suburb of Dallas, a few miles outside the city. There was a lot of verbal abuse directed toward the Jayhawks on that trip. Police officers escorted the KU team on and off the basketball court, and all the way back to the airport.

Things didn't get much better for the Jayhawks after defeating Southern Methodist in the opening round. During the regional finals with Oklahoma City, Abe Lemons, the coach at OCU, complained that the officials were protecting Chamberlain. The referee, Al Lightner, who was also the sports editor of the *Oregon Statesman* newspaper, said the Oklahoma City players were deliberately dumping on Chamberlain and that Lemons warned him of trouble if "that big nigger piles onto any of my kids." The Oklahoma City players allegedly referred to Kansas players frequently that way. Lemons denied it, so it's Lightner's word against his.

That was the first and only time during Wilt's career at Kansas that the team was faced with racial problems. There weren't any incidents that I recall as we traveled throughout the Big 8 Conference. During Chamberlain's two years at Kansas we didn't play any games in the South, except for those two tournament games in Dallas.

As was expected, the Jayhawks escaped Dallas by crushing the Oklahoma City team, 81-61, to earn a berth in the Final Four at Municipal Auditorium in Kansas City. With that trip to the Final Four, Kansas became the first team in NCAA history to reach the finals four times (1940, 1952, 1953 and 1957).

Even though the Jayhawks faced defending national champion San Francisco in the semifinal game, the Dons were no match for Wilt and the guys, as Kansas cruised to a 80-56 win. San Francisco had won its first five games that season, but then lost five of its next six. With that win for Kansas, the Jayhawks were set to square off with the North Carolina Tar Heels.

The two teams had reached the title game in very different ways. Kansas had a fairly easy path to the championship, but the road wasn't as easy for Carolina. Despite being undefeated by the time they reached the championship game, the Tar Heels had a triple-overtime battle in the semifinals against Michigan State, winning 74-70. North Carolina was led by Frank McGuire's coaching and their great star player, Lennie Rosenbluth.

It looked like it was going to be a fairly easy Kansas win against the tired Tar Heels, but it obviously wasn't.

McGuire started the game with a gimmick, sending out 5-foot-10 Tommy Kearns for the opening tip against Chamberlain. Frank was trying to throw some strange quirk into the ballgame. It certainly made Wilt think that if Carolina was going to do something stupid like this, what other tricks are they going to employ during the game?

As some of the players who played in the game have said, it was very boring because there wasn't a lot of scoring. Jayhawk player Bob Billings said that the game might have been exciting for the fans because it was so close, but it was boring for the players because the Kansas team wanted to run. Carolina wouldn't. It was so slow that in the second overtime, no points were scored at all. The game came down to the final play in the third overtime.

Kansas was ahead by one point late in the final OT. A foul was called on KU, and the North Carolina player, Joe Quigg, hit both free throws with six seconds left. Kansas, down 54-53, called a timeout at midcourt with a few seconds remaining. Harp's plan was to have the ball inbounded to 6-foot-6 Ronnie Loneski, who could throw it over the defense to Wilt for an "easy" two points and the win. Somehow the North Carolina players trapped Loneski out of position, causing him to make a shaky pass in Wilt's direction. The ball landed in Quigg's hands. The buzzer sounded and the Tar Heels won. It turned out to be a nightmare for Kansas.

It was an amazing game, but a terrible shock to Kansas people. Everybody thought Kansas had the best team in the country, without a doubt, but we didn't win the national championship. The loss was difficult for the Kansas players and coaches, but it may have been toughest on Wilt. The pressure placed on him throughout the season made him feel as though he let the team, and Kansas fans, down by not leading them to the title. Wilt was so down about the loss that after he left Kansas at the end of the next season, he didn't come back to the university for any appearances for 40 years.

Wilt finally returned to Kansas in January of 1998, for the retirement of his jersey No. 13 on a warm and terrific afternoon. It was such an emotional event. In all those years, Wilt had felt that the people of Kansas had resented him for having lost the national championship for KU in 1957. The obvious outpouring of emotion for him, and vice versa, that afternoon dispelled any thoughts that might have existed in his mind about that, and healed any rift there may have been. It was sensational. We are all so grateful that the big guy did come back to Kansas before his untimely death. He will surely be missed.

Jerry Waugh

I never thought the Kansas Jayhawks were going to lose in that championship game to North Carolina in 1957. In our semifinal game with San Francisco, the Dons opened up the game and we beat the blood out of them. That was the first time that the Jayhawks played a team that opened it up. The game was never a contest.

Carolina had played a triple-overtime semifinal game with Michigan State, winning down the stretch, so there was the thought that Kansas would have an easier final. Not to mention the fact that with Wilt Chamberlain on the inside, we didn't feel like we should lose at all during the season.

Much of the Tar Heels' plan that night was based on the gamesmanship of Frank McGuire. For instance, Kansas came out first to warm up before the game, and took a pre-assigned bench which followed NCAA regulations. When Carolina came out on the court, one of its managers brought all of the Tar Heels' equipment down and put it on our bench. Dick Harp stopped him and said he was making a mistake.

1957 Final, North Carolina vs. Kansas

The manager said, "No, no, North Carolina always takes this bench, away from their first half goal." I will never forget that statement. Needless to say, Dick was madder than hell, and talked to tournament director Reeves Peters, who was also the commissioner of our league. The rules of the tournament were preset and Reeves should have gone to the Carolina manager and told them to move to the other bench. Instead, Reeves said, "Dick, they're our guests since we're hosting the tournament. Let them have what they want." So, Dick was upset from the outset.

Frank McGuire never came out to the court before the game. He was the old pro who met with the team when it was ready to play; that was his role. We were of the mind that we were there as a group and as a family.

Most of Frank's players at that time were New Yorkers. He recruited heavily in New York because he was from that area. The tempo of the title game was set up as here are the New York City slickers, coming out to take advantage of the country bumpkins. As a result, that was upsetting to Dick. Frank had a great ball club, but I don't think, with all things being equal, it would be a very difficult team to play against with Chamberlain on our side.

McGuire brought out his gamesmanship for the tip, by having 5-10 guard Tommy Kearns jump center against Chamberlain. Seeing a gag like that to start the game was surprising because we didn't expect it, but kids adjust to things like that pretty quickly. We knew it was all just a big act from the Carolina coach.

Carolina jumped out to an early lead by hitting nearly every shot they threw up, including their free throws. They seemingly didn't miss anything in the early part of the game. Defensively, the Tar Heels had decided that they were going to play a tight zone around Wilt and tie him up. We knew we were in for a long evening.

Once Carolina got that lead early, it controlled the tempo of the game. The thing that we couldn't have happen to us that year with Wilt, but it did against Carolina, was lose control of the game early. It was always a difficult game if the other team got a little bit of a lead in the opening minutes, because they were usually going to hold the ball on offense and stay in a zone on defense, so Wilt wouldn't have a chance to beat them. That's just what Carolina did.

At that particular time in college basketball, Chamberlain was such a dominant player that teams had to go to great lengths to stop him, even if his game wasn't perfect. (Although that was the case throughout Wilt's entire basketball career, not just in college.) He had been such a successful and spectacular player in high school, that he wasn't overly willing to change at the college level. Toward the coaches, he was politely disobedient. Wilt was a great shooter if he could bounce the ball on the floor, turn around and shoot it. Our coaching staff knew that at the college level the defenders weren't going to let him do that, so we wanted him to be able to spin around and go strong toward the basket. Wilt was resistant to that kind of change. Anytime someone tries to change behavior, or change physically how they shoot a ball, they need to realize that there could be some failure along the way. Failure was not an option in Wilt's mind, regardless of the final outcome.

When Chamberlain first came to Kansas, he struggled with his free-throw shooting. He was resistive to changing his technique and working with that one change. As a result, he constantly changed techniques in his free-throw shooting, most of which were a result of his pride in wanting to do well. He was a very proud person. Because of that, he was not willing to stick with changing his game if it meant the possibility of failure; even if, in the long run, the change would have been to his benefit. As I say though, he was polite in his disobedience.

However, I do need to say that Wilt's personality and how it impacted his growth as a player was not a factor in the championship game with North Carolina. Our team's failure to win that game was not based on Wilt's shortcomings by any means, especially considering that in the game he scored 23 points, had 15 rebounds and was selected as the Most Outstanding Player of the tournament. Certainly the Jayhawks' 31.9 percent shooting from the field as a team in that game played a factor in the outcome.

The Carolina game plan in the 1957 title game was to stay in the zone against Wilt, double and triple-teaming him. They had some big, strong kids to move inside against him. When you slow down the tempo of the game, as McGuire's club did, and a shot is open, like we had a few times, you need to effectively shoot it. It was obvious we had the perimeter shots available, but being open so little can cause a player's collar to tighten. When a team is used to running, and the speed of the game is slowed to an unnatural pace, shooters aren't quite as relaxed. We had good perimeter shooters. But, for some reason, they didn't knock down the shots.

Finally in the second half, we were able to creep back into the ballgame and forge a six-point lead. Harp decided that we were going to keep the ball on the perimeter in hopes of bringing the Tar Heels out of their zone. So we started to hold the ball, and would have been content to win by six points, but McGuire sent their guard, Kearns, out to foul our perimeter players. Carolina was willing to trade a free throw for possession. The rules permitted the officials to call a two-shot penalty for intentional fouls, which Kearns' fouls were, but the officials chose not to see it that way. We had good shooters on our team, but darned if they didn't miss their free throws that night. With our misses and Carolina's rebounding, the Tar Heels were able to tie the game late.

The game turned because Kansas was unable to make its free throws. McGuire only sent Kearns out to pressure the Jayhawks on offense, while the rest of the team stayed in that zone around Wilt. The game went into three overtimes.

At the end of the third overtime, we had the final possession, down by one point, with a timeout. Following the timeout our plan was to flash big six-foot-six Ron Loneski at the top of the key, and he was going to throw the ball above the rim so Wilt could just take it and score. Loneski didn't get the pass quite high enough. Today we would use the alley-oop, but the game of basketball hadn't quite evolved to that idea in 1957. Carolina held on for the 54-53 win.

Wilt Chamberlain was a prodigy of the game when he was at Kansas. He always thought that his superior ability could help the Jayhawks win, and that he could carry this team. I don't know whether he took the burden of the loss in the 1957 title game upon himself. Wilt was a very closed, private person, so we never knew exactly how he felt. I do know the loss was terribly disappointing to him because he couldn't single-handedly carry the Jayhawks to a national championship. That in itself was disappointing to him. Later I found out that not winning the title played in his factor to leave the university before his senior season.

It was one of those ballgames that we had no doubt about winning, but to the credit of Carolina, they had a plan and they were able to execute it. We came up short to make it a disappointing game. To this day I'd like to play them again.

Lennie Rosenbluth

The largest thing (no pun intended) about that 1957 title game against Kansas, was the fact that we were playing against the big man in the country, sophomore Wilt Chamberlain. So much was written about Wilt that we were in awe of him before we even got to the game. Some of us watched him in the Jayhawks' semifinal game on Friday night, and he was awesome! Chamberlain had 32 of the 80 points that Kansas scored, as they beat San Francisco, 80-56. We had to respect him, but our players felt that we could beat that Kansas ballclub. We just had to have a good plan because once Kansas got the ball inside, there was no stopping Chamberlain.

Carolina head coach Frank McGuire told us not to let Chamberlain beat us. If the other Jayhawks were going to hit their outside shots and beat us, then that was one thing. So, the plan was to surround Chamberlain inside, and contest the outside shot, but don't go out and play the shooters really tight.

Chamberlain felt he could take that team to the title, and rightly so. There weren't many centers in the game at that time who were seven-feet tall and could move like he could. Wilt was a tremendous athlete. He had a fade-away jump shot which was nearly impossible to defend; then, if he was close enough to the basket, he was going to dunk the ball. We didn't want him to have an earth-shattering dunk against us because that would have brought the crowd into the game. We didn't want him to hit the fade-away, but if he did that, at least the crowd would not be as vocal and alive.

Playing against Chamberlain was tough! Several of us were familiar first-hand with what Wilt was capable of doing because after his senior year of high school, we played against each other in the Catskill Mountains in New York. Wilt was on one hotel team and I was on another. He just ate us up. He was amazing.

At Carolina, we knew what he could do, but in the NCAA title game, it was a matter of whether or not we could stop him from dunking the ball. In those days, to have a man able to go over his defenders and stuff the ball, was unheard of, especially with his type of strength. When you go up against a player who is so domineering inside, and you know that if he gets the ball he's just going to jump over you, it's tough. We tried to keep a man in front of Wilt to discourage Kansas from passing to him. With Chamberlain's athletic ability, it was just a matter of time before they were going to start to get the ball inside.

McGuire told us in a pregame meeting that 5-10 Tommy Kearns was going to jump center against Wilt. In several of the Kansas games throughout the season, Chamberlain would win the tip, break down the middle of the court, get the return pass and have a tremendous dunk, bringing the Kansas crowd into the ballgame. McGuire felt that there was no way we could get the tip anyway, and he especially didn't want Chamberlain to open the championship game with a slam dunk to get the crowd excited, so Kearns jumped center and the rest of us dropped back under the Kansas basket to stop an opening dunk. McGuire instructed Tommy to squat all the way down before the jump to give Chamberlain and the rest of his team something to think about. It looked ridiculous, but Wilt always said that he couldn't figure out what in the world Kearns was doing. McGuire wanted us to have any advantage we could throughout that game.

1957 Final, North Carolina vs. Kansas

Trying to get that upper-hand even caused problems before the game started. Picking the side on which each team would sit became an issue, although I don't know why, since it was supposed to be a neutral court.

Coach would wait in the locker room until it was game time, then he would come out, ready to play, dressed to the hilt. (People today talk about the way coach Pat Riley dresses. McGuire was dressing that way many years before.) As we were warming up, there was a rhubarb and someone punched McGuire. To this day I don't know exactly who did it, but I have an idea (and it wasn't a Carolina person).

Even though I grew up in the Bronx, and there were many good schools in the New York area, it didn't take much coaxing to get me to go south. Originally, out of high school, I thought I had a scholarship to play at North Carolina State where Everett Case was the head coach. When I went down to Raleigh just to visit the campus, the coaches were having open tryouts, which I didn't mind, but I didn't play well. As a result, Case told me to forget about trying to play for the Wolfpack.

Meanwhile, Harry Gotkin, who was Case's main recruiter, was a friend of McGuire. When Case told me to forget about playing there, Harry got mad, left N.C. State, and started recruiting for McGuire. At that time Frank McGuire was about to leave his coaching position at St.

Clyde Lovellette of Kansas was the first player to score 30 or more points (33) in an NCAA title game (1952).

John's and go to either the University of Alabama or North Carolina. I committed to go with McGuire wherever he went. That ended up being Carolina. I have no regrets whatsoever about my decision.

Coach McGuire was great. His whole idea was to treat us like men, and we didn't want to let him down. He was a tremendous coach on using the clock. We would practice game situations such as learning what to do when we were down by five points with three minutes left to play in the game. During the season we never panicked when we were trailing because of all of the practices we had for game situations. Coach McGuire was not an x's and o's type of coach — that was handled by assistant Buck Freeman

McGuire was tremendous at motivating his teams. He got us up to play every ballgame. Largely because of that preparation, we were ready to play the Jayhawks in the championship.

Kansas opened up the game with a box-and-one defense against me, which I always felt was a mistake. The Jayhawks might feel the same way because our team came out and hit its first six shots from outside.

Before Kansas could get out of that defense, we were ahead 19-7. Right away, with the combination of the defensive schemes for both teams, the pressure was put on the outside shooting of the Jayhawks. Since we were falling back on Chamberlain, and they were down by 12 points, the Jayhawks had to hit their outside shots. If we had been down by six or seven points at the beginning, then the whole complexion of the game would have changed. Instead, we had that lead.

We had, for that era, a fairly big ballclub at Carolina. Joe Quigg was 6-8, Pete Brennan was 6-6 and I was 6-5. When teams tried to match up with us, Joe would guard the biggest man, even though he was basically a forward and not a center. Pete would have the second tallest, then, of course, I had the third tallest. Since Joe and Pete played more of a forward position, I would take my man inside the paint. If I had the big man playing against me, I would go outside and let Pete or Joe go inside. We almost forced teams to play a zone against us, which was great because we were an excellent outside shooting team. So, needless to say, we were surprised when Kansas came out in a box-and-one.

As for Chamberlain, he had only two baskets in the first half, but the Jayhawks found a way to get him the ball in the second half. The game stayed close throughout the second half. Even though most people probably thought that we were tired, having played a triple-overtime semifinal game against Michigan State, the way we felt, there was no way Kansas was going to beat us.

McGuire played his starting five a lot, so we were in good shape. In most games, the subs might come in during crucial times, but even then, it only meant one or two other players. Since we were in excellent shape, we weren't really tired going into overtime against Kansas.

Don't get me wrong, we had a great second ballclub. There were times during scrimmages when the second team killed us. They delighted in beating us. Bob Young, Ken Rosemond and Danny Lotz, for instance, were good ballplayers. Coming off the bench they would get key rebounds and crucial points to help us win a game.

After scoring 20 points with Kansas ahead 46-43, I fouled out with 1:47 remaining. Young replaced me and helped tie up the game. I always felt that someone on our team would step forward for the win. That night it was Joe Quigg.

At the end of the third overtime, Quigg went to the free-throw line and put us ahead with less than a minute to play. Kansas called a time-out to figure out how to get the ball to Wilt Chamberlain. Everybody in the arena knew that the ball was going to Wilt. Again, we decided that if the Jayhawks were going to win the ballgame on that last play, they were going to have to take an outside shot. If Chamberlain had gotten the ball, he could have either dunked it or been fouled. Neither of those two options would have been good. As the pass went toward Chamberlain, as expected, Quigg tipped the ball.

There was a lot of pressure for Ron Loneski in that situation, in that type of ballgame to get the pass into Chamberlain. With six seconds left in the game, not only did the pass have to be perfect, but Wilt would have had to do something with the ball quickly. I would have been surprised if Chamberlain had been able to get the ball and make a move toward the basket, because all of the Tar Heels were ready to swarm him.

Years later, we used to see Wilt Chamberlain and have dinner with him at his restaurant in Boca Raton, Fla. That championship game bugged him more than any other game in his entire career. He'd tell me, "You know, we should have beaten you guys."

"Big guy,"I'd reply, "you know, you're right." There was really no way we should have been able to beat a man of his size, strength and athletic ability.

We heard reports after the game that we were a 12 point underdog, despite going into the game with a 31-0 record. We couldn't believe it! We are probably the only undefeated No. 1 team in history to go into the title game as the underdog. Besides having Chamberlain, people also felt that Kansas had an advantage over us because the game was being played in the Jayhawks' backyard, Municipal Auditorium in Kansas City. The few Carolina fans who were at that game, probably fewer than 100 people, were sitting near the top of the upper deck; it was difficult to hear anyone clapping for Carolina.

Our whole plan, basically, was to take good shots and hold the ball. Our North Carolina team made very few turnovers during that year. McGuire had a motto all season that the ball is gold and you don't throw away gold. So, we played a possession-type game, not a slow-down game but a possession game. It was a matter of making sure that we didn't turn the ball over.

Then, by holding Wilt to just six field goals (with his 11-16 free-throw shooting, he still ended the night with 23 points), we kept the crowd silent most of the game. When the game was over, there was an eerie, dead silence in Municipal Auditorium. It was weird.

Any player who ever played in a Final Four will remember it for the rest of his life. Even back in the late 1950s, without nationwide television and all of the hype that is associated with the Final Four today, it was a fantastic event. In Kansas, everybody knew what the game was about and what it meant, but it wasn't like that around the entire country. Fans in Kansas City stopped us in the streets and talked to us. It really was something.

I will always remember what a great experience it was to go to Kansas City. North Carolina was the only Atlantic Coast Conference school to reach the NCAA championship game (another Carolina team played for the 1946 title), and we were the first ACC team to win the national championship. It was a thrill to be undefeated and go that far in the tournament. We were experiencing plenty of firsts throughout the entire season.

Once we reached the No. 1 spot in the nation, and were on our way to the Final Four, the press started following us quite a bit. That was a new experience for us at Carolina (certainly now they do it all the time there). Back then the school didn't have any type of basketball reputation.

Despite all of the new attention, and our quest for an undefeated season, we never felt any pressure at all during the year. The coaches had the pressure, and the fans may have felt pressure, but we were relaxed.

Besides the two games in the Final Four, we had many close calls that season. The South Carolina game on the road was a close one where we went into overtime before winning by four points. Then, we

The 1989 national championship game between Michigan and Seton Hall was the 1,500th game in the history of the NCAA Tournament.

were basically beaten at Maryland. All the Terrapins had to do was make their foul shots. In fact, McGuire called a timeout with less than a minute to go in the game and told us, "The streak is over. When the buzzer goes off, go over there and shake their hands because they played a great ballgame."

The Terrapins missed their foul shots, we tied the game up and sent it to overtime. We out-lasted Maryland through two overtimes to win, 65-61. After that Maryland game, people became believers in our team. Certainly McGuire became a believer in what we could do. We played Wake Forest four times, each game was a very close one.

Forget about going undefeated, though. How many players end their college careers by not losing the last game of the season? It has always been a thrill for me to think about that 1957 season, especially knowing that we played against a good Kansas team with Wilt Chamberlain.

With the success we enjoyed that season, we like to think of ourselves as the forerunners to what the Carolina teams are doing today, and certainly the ACC. A lot of positive things happened for the University and the state of North Carolina because we went to Kansas City and won the national championship.

1957 Final, North Carolina vs. Kansas

Most people know that Dean Smith played at the University of Kansas in the early 1950s, and later became an assistant under McGuire before taking over as the Carolina head coach after the 1961 season, but people don't know that McGuire first met Dean on our trip to the championship in Kansas City. In 1958 he joined McGuire at Carolina. If we had not gone to Kansas City that year, then it may have been a question mark as to whether or not Dean Smith would ever have ended up at Carolina. Would McGuire have known about Coach Smith? There are a lot of ifs involved.

Because of our win, ACC games started being televised locally in the southeast. Kids became more interested in playing high school basketball throughout the state of North Carolina. A lot of people credit our being undefeated and winning the national championship for creating national interest in the UNC basketball program, and legitimizing the ACC as a powerful basketball conference. There were several behind-the-scenes things happening such as these that we didn't know about until years later as a result of our 1957 title.

Part II: The '60s

CHAPTER 3

Kansas City, Missouri
March 20-21, 1964

In the early 1960s, the NCAA was in need of a team to take the national tournament to a new level. Little did anyone know that the program to take it to that next level, UCLA, was about to win its first of 10 championships in 12 years, under legendary head coach John Wooden.

The team that the Bruins had to get past in that 1964 semifinal was the Kansas State Wildcats. The Wildcats, coached by Tex Winter, had an advantage of playing close to home at Municipal Auditorium in Kansas City.

Kansas State kept the game close throughout, and actually led with a couple of minutes remaining, but couldn't hold off the Bruins' final run. Some people, especially K-State fans, point to one key for the Bruins ... the UCLA cheerleaders. For whatever reason, the UCLA cheerleaders did not show up at Municipal Auditorium until the last few minutes of the game when K-State had the lead. Legend has it that when the cheerleaders entered the arena, a Wildcat player missed a layup that would have iced the game for Kansas State.

In his 15 seasons at Kansas State, Winter took six of his Wildcat teams to the NCAA tournament. Since leaving the college game in 1983, he has enjoyed success in the National Basketball Association as an assistant to Phil Jackson with the Chicago Bulls and now the Los Angeles Lakers.

1964 All-Tournament Team	Final Four Participants
Bill Buntin, Michigan	Duke
Gail Goodrich, UCLA	Kansas State
Walt Hazzard, UCLA	Michigan
(Most Outstanding Player)	UCLA
Jeff Mullins, Duke	
Willie Murrell, Kansas State	

National Semifinals	National Championship
Duke 91, Michigan 80	UCLA 98, Duke 83
UCLA 90, Kansas State 84	

Tex Winter

First off, when reading through this story about the 1964 season and the UCLA-Kansas State games, keep in mind that it is from a slanted view. I certainly have to admit that I am biased toward the Wildcats.

The interesting thing about the 1964 tournament was that the Final Four teams were UCLA, Michigan, Duke and Kansas State, which was the same order of the national rankings, except for K-State which was ranked No. 12. Before the tournament started, I had a feeling we would slip past some teams. We were only ranked 12th in the nation despite really playing well (winning our last 12 games of the season) and we also had an uncanny ability to break the press that I thought would help.

One of the highlights for us during the tournament was facing Wichita State in the Midwest Regional Finals in Wichita, Kan. The Wheat Shockers were heavily favored, but we beat them by eight points, 94-86, to earn a trip to the Final Four. Wichita State had what they thought was one of the best presses in the nation and we riddled them. Actually, one of the reasons I think we won that game against the Shockers was because they did try to press us. Most everybody wanted them to beat us because they were rated 4th in the country ... that would have given the Final Four the top four teams in the nation. I'm glad we spoiled that scenario.

Our Final Four opponent, UCLA, had that devastating press that all the teams in the country feared so much. We really relished the idea of

35

playing against that, especially after breaking through the press that Wichita State threw at us. Even without their exhaustive pressure defense, UCLA had a very well-balanced basketball team. Walt Hazzard was the ball handler and the initiator of their offense. We did an excellent job on him and gave him a lot of problems. Fred Slaughter, out of Topeka, Kan., was their center. Gail Goodrich, a left-hander, was their best shooter. They also featured Jack Hirsch and Keith Erickson.

We had played them earlier in the season, a couple of weeks before Christmas, in what was called The Sunflower Classic. UCLA and the University of Southern California came out to Kansas to play us and the Kansas Jayhawks. The way the Classic was supposed to work was that we would play UCLA in Manhattan one night, then play USC in Lawrence the next night. Kansas would play USC in Manhattan and UCLA in Lawrence. That season the Bruins were the headlining team nationally, so in the Classic, the idea was to let the two teams from Kansas play UCLA in front of their own crowd. Since USC didn't have nearly the team or draw as UCLA, we weren't concerned about playing them in Lawrence instead of Manhattan.

Evidently, as the headlining team, UCLA was able to call their shots and change the schedule for the Classic. As I understand it, J.D. Morgan, the athletic director at UCLA, wouldn't let the Bruins come out unless the games were switched to where they played us in Lawrence and Kansas in Manhattan. That really gave UCLA a big advantage by giving them the home court crowd knowing the rivalry between KU and K-State. The Wildcats aren't too popular in Lawrence, regardless of who they're playing, and the same holds true for the Jayhawks in Manhattan. That switch gave the Bruins a tremendous edge against both us and the Jayhawks. During the two day event, UCLA beat us by three points in Lawrence, then beat Kansas by 20 in Manhattan.

In my mind there was a sense of payback when K-State and UCLA met in the NCAA Tournament, because I wasn't too happy about the switching of opponents that took place in December.

UCLA, with their vaulted press, jumped out to an early lead against us in the 1964 semifinal game. They securely stayed ahead of us until late in the first half when we caught up. The Bruins led 43-41 at the intermission.

Neither team could build a commanding lead in the second half. With less than five minutes to play in the game, we had a five-point lead. I thought we had them on the ropes, because at that point, being ahead, we forced them out of using their press on every possession.

We had the ball, broke the Bruins press, and Jeff Simons, one of the Wildcat guards, missed a 15-foot jump shot that rolled all the way around the rim, started to drop, then came out. Had that shot gone in, we might have had a big enough lead with about a minute to play that UCLA wouldn't have been able to overcome it. But the shot didn't fall, and they came back to beat us, 90-84. Even though we did a decent job containing Hazzard and Goodrich, Erickson scored 28. Coming off the bench, Kenny Washington hurt us by hitting some big baskets on his way to 13 points. UCLA had a great team; there's no taking anything away from them, even though we had our chances to win.

On a side note, the UCLA cheerleaders (those beautiful, California gals in those short skirts that people in the Midwest weren't used to seeing) were delayed getting to the game for some reason. Late in the ballgame, while

Final Four® Fast Facts Kansas coach Dick Harp became the first person to play in an NCAA championship game (Kansas, 1940) and later coach the same school in the NCAA Finals (1957).

UCLA was still down, these cheerleaders came storming in Kansas City's Municipal Auditorium. According to some of the reports in the paper, they felt the entrance of the cheerleaders was the spark that ignited the Bruins victory. (I thought it had more to do with the officiating, myself.)

The Kansas State game was the closest call for UCLA in the Final Four that year. They came back the next night and clobbered Duke, 98-83, for the championship and an undefeated season.

Michigan beat us the next night in the third-place game. The Wolverines were big and strong physically, with Cazzie Russell as their playmaker. The third-place game is sometimes a tough game to play, especially after playing a disappointing game the night before. We definitely didn't play well against them.

That 1964 title was the start of UCLA's incredible run in the Final Four. I've often thought that had coach Johnny Wooden not won that first one, his run of 10 titles in 12 years might not have started. The next one might have been more difficult for them.

John Wooden

I would suspect that every coach who has won a national championship would agree that the first one is extremely important. That is why 1964 sticks out for us. For our program however, I began to see the light of day during our first trip to the Final Four in 1962 when we lost to Cincinnati, 72-70, in the final seconds of the game. We had the ball late with the score tied, but lost possession on an offensive foul. Cincinnati went down the court and scored. Even though we didn't win the championship that season, the experience was a kickoff to give our players the feeling that we could possibly compete for a national championship.

The next year, 1963, I started using the zone press, which I had used successfully while teaching at Indiana State and in high school at South Bend Central High School. I hadn't used it since arriving at UCLA in 1948, but in 1963 we had the material that was well suited for that defense. That season we lost in the regionals of the NCAA Tournament to Arizona State, a team that shot the ball as well as I have ever seen a team shoot in a game.

We had all of those UCLA players back for the 1964 season, following a year in which the team had improved throughout the entire year. Having the same players back who had worked on the zone press for a season, was crucial. They played extremely well. That was one of the best pressing teams we ever had, and certainly one of the best I have ever seen. We went through the season undefeated at 30-0.

In many games that year we would be behind early, but our press would almost always take effect sooner or later. That is what happened in the game against Kansas State, and it happened again in the championship against Duke. Our zone press defense was one of the main keys to our success for that entire season, and throughout our next nine titles.

That first championship also sparked a chain of events which helped us win those nine additional championships. Recruiting after that 1964 national championship was tremendous. Winning in the Final Four the first time made recruiting easier, then when we repeated as champions the next year, getting players was so much different. We also got a new place to play after winning those first championships which helped tremendously. Lew Alcindor would never have come to UCLA had it not been for the new Pauley Pavilion, nor would he have come had we not won in 1964 and 1965. Those years attracted his attention. It made UCLA one of the five schools he wanted to visit.

After we beat Duke in the championship game in 1964, Alcindor's high school coach called me and said that he and Lewis had watched that game together on television, and after we won, UCLA was one of the five schools Lewis wanted to visit the next year. We would have never attracted his attention if we hadn't won. When we repeated as champions the next year, which was Alcindor's senior year, that solidified his decision. Then he saw what is, in my mind, the best college basketball arena on the West Coast, and realized how he was going to dedicate it by playing the very first game (I pointed that out, you know), he knew the decision was a good one. I never visited Alcindor during recruiting – I did very little recruiting anyway.

A winning tradition certainly helps with recruiting. There are a lot of good players that don't want to go to schools that haven't done well. Since we were winning in the early 1960s, players wanted to come to school at UCLA. It being the first championship for our program, and the one that started our NCAA championship tradition, makes the 1964 title very memorable.

CHAPTER 4

College Park, Maryland
March 18-19, 1966

At the time, the 1966 championship game between Kentucky and Texas Western (now called the University of Texas-El Paso, or UTEP) was mainly seen as a regular national championship game. Since that time, in which the Miners won 72-65, the game is more widely seen for its racial significance. Texas Western was a team that featured an all-black starting five against Kentucky's all-white starting lineup, coached by Adolph Rupp.

Opponents of that idea, such as Larry Conley, a senior starter on that Kentucky team, say the players saw the game as just that ... a game. Conley points out that players on both sides of the court saw it as a game of Texas Western against Kentucky, not black against white. Several well-respected journalists and coaches agree with Conley. Possibly the main reason the game has been seen that way is because of Rupp, who many consider to be an "old Southerner" (even though he was from Kansas). After all, had it been Duke, also an all-white team, instead of Kentucky, would it still be considered such a significant game?

"Rupp's Runts," as that Kentucky team was called, with no players over six-foot-five, were not ranked in any preseason polls, but finished the season with an impressive 27-2 record. Conley was the passing specialist on that team, leading the Wildcats in assists during his three varsity seasons.

After finishing his collegiate career, Conley played one season with the Kentucky Colonels of the old ABA. Today, Conley is a college basketball analyst for several networks.

1966 All-Tournament Team

Jerry Chambers, Utah
   (Most Outstanding Player)
Louie Dampier, Kentucky
Bobby Joe Hill,
   Texas Western (now UTEP)
Jack Marin, Duke
Pat Riley, Kentucky

Final Four Participants

Duke
Kentucky
UTEP
Utah

National Semifinals

Kentucky 83, Duke 79
UTEP 85, Utah 78

National Championship

UTEP 72, Kentucky 65

Larry Conley

Heading into preseason, 1965-1966, our Kentucky team was not ranked in anyone's poll. We had come off of a bad year in 1965. We finished 15-10, and we never really played well. The obvious question was why would anyone want to pick a team for the top 25 that didn't have a player over 6-foot-6, and had lost two of the main players from the previous year? Needless to say, not many people expected us to make any noise in the Southeastern Conference, let alone the NCAA Tournament. Because of our lack of size, we earned the nickname "Rupp's Runts." Three of our starters on that team, Pat Riley, Louie Dampier and Tommy Kron, played professional basketball and the fourth, Thad Jaracz, could have, but didn't.

After a surprisingly good regular season and a run in the NCAA Tournament, which included defeating Duke in the national semifinals, we were set to meet a solid Texas Western team for the national championship. Who would have thought that Rupp's Runts and Texas Western would have been in the finals, but the Miners had a tough team.

A misconception that people have about that game is that we viewed our semifinal game with Duke as the national championship game. After our win over the Blue Devils we sat and watched the Texas Western-Utah game. Utah only featured one highly skilled player, Jerry Chambers. (He was named the Most Outstanding Player of the tournament.)

41

During the regular season, both us and Texas Western had won our first 23 games before losing. The very day that we received our first loss of the season, March 5, to Tennessee, Texas Western lost at Seattle. Going into that day, we were No. 1 in the country and they were No. 2. If they had defeated Seattle while we lost to Tennessee, they in all probability would have become the No. 1 team. Instead, we stayed at the top of the polls, Duke moved up from No. 3 to No. 2, and Texas Western moved down to No. 3. Because we knew how good Texas Western was, we didn't look at the semifinal game with Duke as our national championship. It's not like the Miners had ascended from a cave out of nowhere ... a team doesn't achieve the No. 3 ranking unless it has good players and excellent coaching.

In the title game, Texas Western jumped ahead of us quickly, taking a 7-2 lead. We started pressing a bit, and missed our first couple of shots. It was evident to me right from the beginning that we needed to make some quick alterations. Texas Western played a straight man-to-man defense the entire game. So, one of the things we tried to do offensively was draw my defender, Harry Flournoy, who was considerably smaller than me, inside the lane. I attempted to post him up and get a couple of easy baskets and swing the flow of the game in our direction. The first time we tried that I got the ball at the free-throw line, turned to shoot and was hit on the elbow by Flournoy. The ball went all the way over the backboard. I turned to the official and said, "I'm not that bad of a shot. I don't shoot the ball over the top of the basket from the free-throw line." He just said, "No foul. No foul." That's when I knew we were going to have a long night.

Our inability to get our offense started really hurt us. I give Miner head coach Don Haskins a lot of credit for this, because he took us out of our offense. There is some irony here. For the first time in Kentucky coach Adolph Rupp's career he put in a new offense in October and November when we first started the year. That offense would have been perfect for what we were trying to do against Texas Western. They started picking us up at midcourt and we just couldn't get into our normal flow. The new offense we had practiced early in the season would have helped us get things going by extending the offense.

The irony is this ... we were beating teams so badly at the beginning of the year that we didn't have to implement the new scheme. So, instead of working on that offense as much as we did in November, we basically let it go away and didn't use it at all during the season. It would have been perfect to use against Texas Western, but none of us thought about it. I was one of the captains of the team that year, and I was trying to figure out ways we could beat Texas Western's pressure defense, but

I never thought to install the new offense.

We never got in sync that night. Texas Western's defense was very tough on us. People thought that we were intimidated because Texas Western had players who could dunk, but that didn't bother us. Having a team with no players taller than 6-foot-6, as was our case, our opponents were dunking on us regularly. It was no big deal; a team dunked, got two points, we got the ball and went the other way.

A player or team has to make compensations for inadequacies. One of our obvious shortfalls (pardon the expression) was size. What do you do to overcome the size deficit that you face? You run a lot and move the ball around the court quickly to open people who can shoot. Since we didn't have a big guy inside to slow us down, our compensation was moving the ball, which forced us to become a very good passing team. I was more renowned than anybody on that team for my passing because Coach Rupp always told me to get the ball to Riley or Dampier to shoot. It wasn't as if I was a poor shooter, because I had my nights, but Pat and Louie were excellent shooters, and they carried our team offensively during the season. Kron could shoot, but the other two could be deadly. Even our 6-foot-5 1/2 post player, Jaracz, had a strange, running left-handed hook shot that was great. All of us had a little something we could contribute and I guess mine was passing.

As a year goes on, players on a team begin to develop a bonding and an understanding of what they're going to do, where they're going to do it, and when they're going to do it. We almost had a sixth sense of each other's thoughts. For instance, if I had the ball on a 3-on-2 break, I knew Riley and Dampier were not going to the basket, but rather to a corner, so I would kick it to a corner if they were on either side of me. They would drain that jump shot like clockwork. If I had Kron or Jaracz with me, I knew they were going to take it to the basket.

The really good teams have that unspoken ability to communicate. They understand what their teammates are capable or not capable of doing. It sounds strange to say that, but there really is a non-verbal communication that goes on between the players when they're on the floor. Look at the clubs that are struggling and chances are they don't communicate very well with each other.

We didn't have many chances in the 1966 Finals to use that unspoken communication. When it was all said and done that night, we suffered a disappointing 72-65 loss.

Over the past 30-plus years, a huge deal has been made about the racial overtones of that game with our all-white Kentucky team against Texas Western's all-black starting five. The racial situation of that game was never discussed by our team. Absolutely not! Period. All of the talk about it seems to be after the fact. It's almost as if people thought we had never played against black players, but all of us on that Kentucky team grew up playing against black players.

What continues to puzzle me is how people continue to maintain the alleged social importance of that 1966 title game. The overall social upheaval at that time was unprecedented in this country, unless you went back to the era of the Great Depression. Groups and individuals appeared to be pitted against each other in the 1960s. The Voting Rights Act was signed in 1964, the Vietnam War was getting started in a big way, college campuses around the country were in turmoil ... there was a lot of anger out there.

Demonstrations were a symbol of that time period. Students demonstrated on our Lexington campus, and I knew some of those people and liked them. When I was asked to participate in those demonstrations, I declined. My goal was to get a college education, get out of school and get on with my life. I didn't need extra distractions.

As far as the racial implications and social issues involved in 1966, those never entered our game. I have talked to a couple of the Texas Western players over the years and they have said the same thing ... that it was just a basketball game. The thing that caused all of the flack was Coach Rupp's presence because he was a man in his 60s in the twilight of his coaching career, a throwback to the "Old South" (even though he was from Kansas) and he had an all-white team.

There were a couple of national reporters who didn't care a lot for Coach Rupp and they were less interested in reporting the facts of the game and more interested in discussing the fact that an all-white team had played a team with a starting five that was all-black. It

Final Four. Fast Facts

In 1991, Duke coach Mike Krzyzewski became the first coach since John Wooden to take a school to four straight Final Fours. This was his, and Duke's, first title.

wasn't the fact of a team with an all-black starting five playing an all-white team as much as it was the aura of Kentucky, white, the old coach and the "old ways," playing against Texas Western. The players had absolutely nothing to do with this issue. To this day, a couple of those national reporters still don't believe me. That 1966 Kentucky-Texas Western game had more social significance after it was over than it did while it was being played.

Obviously, I'm glad we beat Duke in the semis, but it would have been interesting to see if this furor about the racial differences would have been made had Duke been playing Texas Western. Duke also had an all-white team. Would the same things about Coach Rupp and the game have been written if it had been Duke and Texas Western? Sure, on the court Coach Rupp was verbally tough on his players, demanding a lot of his teams and himself. I don't have a problem with a coach demanding a lot from his players if he also is working as hard as he can to be good. However, just because Coach Rupp was tough on his teams, and had an all-white team in Kentucky in the mid-1960s does not mean he was a racist.

Coach Rupp was a driven man. Success was very important to him. Had he been a CEO of a company and not a coach, that corporation would have been just as successful as his teams. When we traveled he read the *Wall Street Journal* instead of the sports page. He was a very bright man with a master's degree from Columbia.

He also had all sorts of idiosyncrasies and superstitions which we used to play up. For instance, he used to think that finding a hair pin on the day of a game was important, so we would drop hair pins for him to find. He carried a four-leaf clover and wore a brown suit on the day of a game.

From a player's perspective, I always thought Coach Rupp was fair, despite being a strong disciplinarian. He gave his players the opportunity to succeed. When he put us on the court, he planted the seed in the back of our minds that if we didn't do what was expected of us, there was someone else who was going to take our place. There was always that pressure to perform.

One example of the type of discipline we encountered could be seen on our road trips. Whenever we were at our pregame meal on the road, Coach would eat with us. It was a standing rule that we didn't pick up our forks until Coach Rupp picked up his fork to eat. When he began to eat, then we could all eat. That was the rule, so we just sat there and waited until he was ready to sit down and start eating.

Our practices, particularly the scrimmages, were much tougher than our games. We ran the drills over and over again until we were sick of them. Frankly, practice was boring, but that repetition helped us perform better once we were on the court in a game situation. Before that 1966 season, Coach Rupp had us work harder than during any of my preseasons as a Wildcat, and I think that helped spawn our team's success that year.

For the first time in Coach Rupp's career, we were out there doing preseason two-a-day practices. We had never done that before. By the time the first game rolled around, we were in such great shape that we could blow everyone away, which we did. That was also the first year that we had an intensive running and weightlifting program. Joe B. Hall had just started as an assistant to Coach Rupp, and he brought in this fitness program, and it killed me. I had never been in such great shape as I was before that season. We started running the very first day we got to school and continued right up until the first day of practice. By the time practice started, we could run through drills without the threat of being sore. I've told Joe that throughout the first 10 days of that running program, I probably threw up eight of those days. I finally just quit eating lunch so I wouldn't leave it on the track.

Even though those practices were excruciating at times, our starting five stuck together ... not everyone survived under Coach Rupp's regime. He ran off a lot of players during his tenure as head coach, including seven or eight in my career. Even for the hundreds of guys who stuck it out with him through that program, there were times that we would get so mad at him that we could have killed him; he could be so tough. Yet, when I look upon those days, like anything good that you experience, I have more good feelings than negative ones. Now, decades later, the time is a blur.

There was also a compassionate side to Coach Rupp that most people don't write about. For instance, he was very involved with Cardinal Hill Hospital for Children in Lexington. He gave them money and always went over there at Christmas-time. He could be a very charitable man.

Unfortunately for us, we couldn't give him the national championship. Kentucky's loss to Texas Western, in 1966, may have been one of the toughest in Coach Rupp's career. As far as coaching is concerned, 1966 was late in his life, and he wasn't sure how many more times he could return to a national championship game. That's probably the main reason that loss was so difficult for him. He knew that his coaching days were numbered.

(Before Rupp retired in 1972, he had one other club that was much better than our "Rupp's Runts." The 1968 team with Dan Issel and Mike Pratt lost in the regional finals in Lexington to a really good Ohio State club. That Kentucky team was a heck of a group. That was the last time Rupp had a good chance of going back to the title game.)

Say what you will, but to win a national championship, yes, a team needs to have talent and good coaching, but they have to have a little four-leaf clover in their pocket, too. It takes a little bit of luck to get to the championship game. There are probably some teams that have won a title who would admit that.

When we got back to Lexington after losing to the Miners, there was an overwhelming welcome home reception at Memorial Coliseum for us from students and other fans. The one prevalent item that stood out throughout the whole 1966 season with our team was the incredible fan support. They really look to UK to give them something to brag about;

something of pride. That is one of the reasons the program is tradition-ally as strong as it is.

One explanation as to why athletic programs in certain parts of the country have dominated is because the people in those states have such a love for their university and a desire for something to be proud of, that they really go out of their way to make the program successful. Kentucky basket-

Final Four Fast Facts

Municipal Auditorium in Kansas City has played host to more NCAA Championship games (nine) than any other venue.

ball is one of those situations. Arkansas basketball and football, and Nebraska football are similar. In those areas there is nothing else in the state to draw fans away from the university. After we won our first six or seven games in 1966, the state got caught up in our success. People started talking about this "small, little white team." The combination of hard work and the state's pride in our program was crucial to our pros-perity.

Talking to a group like we had that day at the coliseum is something that is better appreciated later in life. I was chosen to speak for the team, but I didn't have a full appreciation of that task. How could I when we had just lost the national championship game? I was despondent for a week, keeping in mind that my last collegiate game was a loss in the title game. I knew I wasn't good enough to play professional basketball, and I had to get on with my life, so that was the end of my competitive playing days.

The only thing I would ever change in my life is that one game ... I would love to have that game back. Obviously that isn't going to happen, and it shouldn't because Texas Western outplayed us that night in 1966.

CHAPTER 5

Los Angeles, California
March 22-23, 1968

After suffering a disappointing loss in the Houston Astrodome at the hands of the Houston Cougars, the UCLA Bruins had looked forward, even if quietly, to another possible meeting with the Cougars during the 1967-1968 season. They got that opportunity in the NCAA semifinals in Los Angeles.

During the first meeting that season between the two clubs, UCLA's star center, Lew Alcindor (later changed to Kareem Abdul-Jabbar), was not at full-strength after being scratched in the eye three games earlier. He ended up having his worst shooting game as a Bruin, hitting just four of 18 shots from the field. The Cougars were led by power forward Elvin Hayes who led all scorers with 39 points.

Roles were somewhat reversed in the semifinal game as UCLA's diamond-and-one defense held Hayes to three-for-10 shooting, while Alcindor scored 19 points on 50-percent shooting from the field.

That was the second-straight season that head coach Guy Lewis and the Houston Cougars made an appearance in the Final Four. Lewis later took three straight teams to the Final Four from 1982-1984.

After a Hall of Fame career in the National Basketball Association, Kareem Abdul-Jabbar is remaining as busy as ever with raising his kids, acting and writing. His latest book, *A Season on the Reservation*, chronicles his time working with a high school team on a White Mountain Apache Indian Reservation. Abdul-Jabbar also has a motivational book set to be released later in 2000. He is considered by many to be one of the best-ever to play college basketball.

Kareem Abdul-Jabbar

We had defeated Houston in the semifinals of the NCAA Tournament in 1967, which probably helped set up all of the attention, and all of the focus, in the 1968 regular-season game between the two schools in the Astrodome. A lot of people had expected Houston to beat us in that 1967 game, but they didn't. Then, Houston's Elvin Hayes didn't have a

1968 All-Tournament Team

Lew Alcindor, UCLA
  (Most Outstanding Player)
Lucius Allen, UCLA
Larry Miller, North Carolina
Lynn Shackelford, UCLA
Mike Warren, UCLA

Final Four Participants

Houston
North Carolina
Ohio State
UCLA

National Semifinals

North Carolina 80, Ohio State 66
UCLA 101, Houston 69

National Championship

UCLA 78, North Carolina 55

lot to say except that he didn't think I was that good of a player. So there was some hype and some challenges thrown around before our game in the Astrodome.

Before the match-up in Houston, I had missed our previous two games after being scratched in my left eye against California. I still suffered from double-vision and blurring when we met the Cougars, but that didn't matter ... there was no way I was going to miss that game in the Astrodome. As a result of the vision problem, and my lack of practicing and conditioning over the previous eight days, I had my worst shooting game as a Bruin in the Houston game, finishing four-for-18 from the field.

Other than that, there really is no reason why we should have lost to Houston except for the fact that we just didn't play our best that day. There was a huge crowd, but it wasn't all that intimidating. The atmosphere was almost surreal around the court because there were more than 50,000 people there, but the floor was out by second base, which meant there were no spectators within 30 yards of the court itself. It was like playing out on a prairie someplace. It was very strange.

As players, we were very disappointed that we lost that game because we felt everyone was watching, and we wanted to be at the very top of our game. Therefore, we were very disappointed when we weren't at the level on which we were capable of playing. Losing that game did give us the incentive to raise our sights and make sure that we would be at our best if we got another shot at the Cougars.

The team felt that with me at 100 percent, and everybody else ready to play, we could beat Houston. That was something, though, that we had to prove on the court. The opportunity to show that we were the better team came in the national semifinals. In terms of willpower, there was no way they were going to beat us in that game. Sure, things could have gone in their favor on the court, but nothing went in their favor. We were ready for everything. That was evident on the court.

Our team didn't really do anything differently to prepare for Houston the second time around. We knew what it was that beat us. This time we were prepared to make the Cougars beat us a different way. UCLA head coach John Wooden helped give us the confidence to know that we were not going to lose to Houston again.

Coach Wooden really understood how to coordinate people's talents. He knew who to put into what spot. He was great at sensing how effective of a player you could be based on your position on the court. It was easy playing for Coach as long as we accepted his guidance. The only guys who ever had a problem with Coach were the ones who felt they knew more than he did or thought things should be done differently on the court than what he was doing.

Every time we listened to what he had to say, and worked hard at what he told us to do, we were successful. That knowledge that he had is one reason I wanted to play at UCLA. As a high school player in New York, I sought Coach Wooden out... like they say in the movie *Field of Dreams*, "If you build it, they will come." Any smart basketball player could see that if he played for Coach Wooden, he might learn a thing or two.

Winning is the most effective way of recruiting. When Coach claims that he didn't recruit, he's putting one on you, because in a big way he placed the idea out to the public that he knew what he was doing by winning championships. He didn't have to blow any horns or shoot any flares to get a high school player's attention. He didn't miss anything when it comes to evaluating players.

Houston had a tough time figuring out how they were going to beat us in the Final Four. The semifinal game really wasn't much of a contest at all. Our press was too much for them ... we really suffocated them with it to where they could really never get into their offense. We did a much better job this game defensively on Elvin.

Hayes was a very physical player and a great rebounder. His turn-around jumper was a tough shot to defend. You had to play good defense against Elvin and get him out of position in order to play effectively against him. Elvin's strong point was that once he got the ball, he would just shoot over everybody, but if you played good denial defense on him and forced him out further to get the ball initially, it really limited his effectiveness. That's basically what we did by using a diamond-and-one defense.

1968 Semifinal, UCLA vs. Houston

In this defense, Lynn Shackelford played straight up man-to-man against Hayes. The rest of us were playing a zone defense. There was a big gap in our defense at the free-throw line, then my area of the zone was down low.

Any time Elvin tried to take Shackelford down low, Lynn would front Hayes and I would trap him from behind ... they couldn't get the lob pass over the top to Hayes. Mike Warren, who was a great athlete, would sometimes sneak in and play defense in the gap at the free-throw line and chase the ball out. That really worked well, because Houston never could figure out how to effectively attack us without Elvin. They needed to position the ball better and do other things ... they just couldn't make the adjustment in time. That frustrated their main offensive front, and took them out of their game. We held Elvin to 10 total points in the game and, as a result, won easily, 101-69.

After beating Houston that soundly, North Carolina was no problem in the championship game. The Tar Heels didn't have much of a chance against us because of the fact that we weren't going to be denied the title. We weren't. 78-55.

That was our second of three national championships while I was at UCLA. Winning an NCAA title and a National Basketball Association (NBA) title, of which I was a part of six, are totally different. The NBA title is all about professional life, adulthood and the corporate world. The college title represents a special time. Adolescence and young adulthood are very special in a person's life.

It's not possible to compare the atmosphere, from a player's standpoint, of a Final Four to that of a NBA World Championship. The dynamics of the two are completely different. If you lose one game in the NCAA Tournament, you're done. In professional basketball the teams play seven games to find out who's the best. In college basketball, there can always be a situation like we saw in 1985 where Villanova beat Georgetown. If those two teams played seven times, Georgetown would win five or six. Instead, they played one game, and it was one game where Villanova had everything together. There is no way I can compare the feelings associated with winning the two different types of championships. Each of the titles with which I've been associated are special.

I certainly won't forget going to the Final Four. I will always remember watching college basketball when I was in high school, and how encouraging it was to think about the possibility of continuing my education through the sport and becoming a part of that excitement. The 1968 semifinal game between UCLA and Houston was so important to the fans that being a part of that is almost like being a part of basketball history. That's the most special aspect of that game for me (although it was

Fred White -

broadcaster

The Bruins had broken the game open with Houston. In the second half, Lew Alcindor got the ball on a fastbreak, brought the ball down the middle lane and threw a pass behind his back that was incredible! The arena in Los Angeles just erupted when he made that pass. It was almost as if the Bruins were telling Houston, "We're going to do about anything we want to do to you tonight."

nice to win the game and then the championship).

The experience of losing to Houston in the Astrodome, then coming back to manhandle them in the semifinals, also showed me, by example, more of Coach Wooden's persona. That loss to Houston was the first in my two years as a varsity player for UCLA. Instead of focusing on Houston, or trying to motivate us before we played them again (as if we needed extra motivation), Coach kept us in focus with our team and working our plan to win the rest of our games. Coach's influence has stayed with me throughout my career since leaving UCLA.

I spent time working with a high school on the White Mountain Apache Reservation in Arizona, which is described in my latest book, *A Season on the Reservation*. Coach Wooden provided the principle fount of knowledge for me to use when I coach or teach kids how to play basketball, as I did in Arizona. For his players, Coach had the game broken down into the most simple aspects in terms of what we needed to know and how we needed to do things. One thing built upon the other. People can read about Coach Wooden and his thoughts on the game, but for me and the others who played for him, we heard the lecture and also did the seminar, so to speak. We did it right by actually getting it straight from him.

The funny thing about Coach Wooden's influence on me is that since I haven't had the time to pursue a career in coaching, his effect has been most greatly felt in my attempts as a parent. I have incredible kids who have turned out great; I've got to give Coach Wooden a lot of credit for what he taught me in terms of being a teacher instead of a coach. He showed me how to teach and challenge people under my charge without taking away their spirit and without letting them go hog-wild. There is a certain balance and sacrifice that you have to make sometimes. It was great to be able to get that from Coach firsthand. His influence has really been important to me as a parent.

Coach Wooden is a pretty clever man ... he figured out how to take the two things that he valued most, family and basketball, to do his life's work and the Lord's work. That's not always easy, but he pulled it off. There aren't a whole lot of people who can say that.

John Wooden

I have never come out and said that any one team I had at UCLA was the best. That would be difficult to do considering we had four teams that went completely through the season undefeated (1964, 1967, 1972, 1973), which can't be improved upon. Then we had three teams that lost only one game, including the 1968 team. However, I will say that the 1968 squad would be more difficult to play against than most of the other teams I had at UCLA.

That team would pose more problems than the others because they had all of the ingredients. We had a tremendous big man in Lew Alcindor (later changed to Kareem Abdul-Jabbar), who unquestionably was the best in the country, and led us to three consecutive national championships, which had never been done. That team featured one of the smartest guards that has ever played, Mike Warren. He could do everything, but the main key was his mentality ... he did things that coaches don't teach players, similar to the mental toughness of Larry Bird. On that team I also had a tremendous outside shooting forward, Lynn Shackelford, who shot extremely well from the corner, taking pressure off Alcindor underneath. At the other forward was a rebounder, Mike Lynn, with as fine a pair of hands as any big player I ever had. He didn't have great speed, but he was quick. The other starter was Lucius Allen, a guard, with about every qualification a player could have at the guard position. As a starting five, that would be about as difficult to participate against as any of my teams. In Kenny Heitz, who had been a starting forward in 1967, we had a great sixth man who could fill in at any position.

Our only loss in that 1968 season was against the University of Houston, in the Houston Astrodome, in what some suggest may be the game that brought a little more attention to college basketball. It may have done that. I have been told that it was the widest televised game of any sports activity up to that time. It was the first regular season college basketball game to be televised nationally. There were more than 55,000 people in the Astrodome (52,693 who had paid), which was not a good place to play basketball, really, the way it was set up. The game was a match-up of the No. 1 and No. 2 teams in the country, with both teams going into the game undefeated. It also featured outstanding players Elvin Hayes of Houston and Alcindor.

Playing in front of a big crowd like that was not intimidating for us. My biggest concern was the way the Astrodome was laid out. The way it was set up that night, I was surprised that anybody could shoot well, because they had television spotlights on each basket, shining toward the court. Surprisingly, it was possible to shoot, as Hayes proved by having a phenomenal night with 39 total points, 29 of which were in the first half. I had one player, Allen, shoot pretty well in that game, leading our team with 25 points.

There were a number of players in college basketball who were very difficult to defend, but many of those tough players were not as well known because they never played on championship teams. In my opinion, Hayes' style of play was not as conducive to all his teammates as Alcindor's was to his teammates. Hayes was a great individual performer. There is no question at all about that in my mind. He proved that later in the pros where he was better adapted to play than he was in college ball. Alcindor was not only great as an individual player, but I think he had a much better team concept of the game than Hayes. Again, that's just one fellow's opinion.

The first meeting that year at the Astrodome was more of a spectacle, and gained so much attention because of that and the fact that the teams were ranked No. 1 and 2. As far as being an emotional game, it wasn't for me or for my team, because it was a non-conference game. Since teams had to win their conference to be in the NCAA Tournament, that was always our aim at the beginning of the year. The games outside of the conference, we played a little differently. Today, it seems like all a team needs is 20 wins to get into the tournament; it doesn't make as much difference where they finish in their conference. We didn't place as much emphasis on the games with teams outside of our conference back then.

Unfortunately, Alcindor had been scratched in the eye causing him to miss the preceding two games, and he still had vertical double-vision in the Houston game. We knew he couldn't play well, and he knew it, but he wanted to play. The doctor gave the OK. I think that was the poorest shooting game Lewis had in the 88 games he played for me, hitting four of 18 attempts from the field. Still, we barely lost the very tight game, with Hayes hitting two free throws with 28 seconds left. We failed to get a shot off before the buzzer and Houston won, 71-69.

I felt that if we played them again, with Alcindor healthy, that we'd do very, very well. After a successful NCAA Tournament run, our course was set to meet Houston again. This time it would be in the national semifinals in Los Angeles. There certainly was no need for me to motivate the Bruins. I never believed in getting my teams emotionally aroused much, anyway, but even so there was a natural motivation to beat Houston this time around. When a coach gets a team too emotionally aroused, I think it hurts their performance. I was not a coach who ever used emotion at any time. Our players, because of the media hype leading up to the semifinal game with Houston, were inspired to do real well. And they did.

When we did meet them in the Final Four, we were doing extremely well in the game, leading at one time by 40 points. Perhaps losing in the Astrodome was an incentive ... you never can tell. Our players thought we were better, and they wanted to prove it. With Alcindor in the game at full strength, we showed that we were better.

Coaching Alcindor was wonderful, because he's intelligent — we never had any worries about him as far as his academics. He was an honor student — he realized he was in school primarily to get an education and he never was a problem in any way. (He just caused problems to opponents.) Lewis was well-liked by his teammates because he was unselfish. He was a team player. I told him one time, "You know, if we so desired, Lewis, we could probably design our offense and have you break [Pete] Maravich's all-time scoring record in the NCAA. But if we did that we would never win a championship." He said that he would never want that and I wouldn't have done it anyway. I believe to this day that we could have done that, and he would have broken the record. To have a superstar that is as unselfish, such a team player, as Lewis was, helps make the other players perform that way, too.

Of the unusually tall players, I think Alcindor and Bill Walton were the quickest. Both were very intelligent; both were honor students, academically; and both were very quick. Both accepted my coaching very well. They worked on things to become better. They were never satisfied just because they were big. They were hard workers. There was never a problem on the floor with them at any time. They were always at practice, always early.

Lewis, at that time, would occasionally have migraine headaches. He would maybe go in a dark room and lie down for awhile, but he would come out shortly, and start working hard without being asked.

He was just a wonderful person with whom to work. He was not an introvert, but in many ways the public thought he was one. With his own group of friends he was not an introvert at all.

Behind Alcindor, our team had great balance in the semifinal game with Houston. No one in the starting five had fewer than 14 points, and

Guy Lewis
- Houston coach

Despite what a lot of people think, I don't agree with the idea that Lew Alcindor was the big difference in the outcome of the two games. I think the UCLA coaching staff was the difference. The Bruin staff figured out something before the 1968 semifinals that no other coaching staff had exposed all season ... that we had only one shooter on the team, even though we led the nation in scoring for two years.

UCLA put a box-and-one on Elvin Hayes to shut him down, then the rest of our team shot atrociously. That wasn't a surprise to me because I saw everyday in practice that we didn't have any consistent shooters.

The Bruin people can talk all they want to about how ineffective Alcindor was in the game that we won in the Astrodome, but he hit seven-of-eight free throw attempts so I know he could see the basket. That was just a very emotional game.

Their coaching staff ran a different defense in the semifinals that effectively took Elvin out of his game and it killed us.

no one had more than 19. That was a very memorable game. The game in the Astrodome was memorable only because of the immense crowd, and the way the court sat out in the middle of this huge place. We were quite a ways from the fans and the rest of the stadium. One of my players had to go to the bathroom, and it took him about a half hour ... it seemed like it was a quarter-mile from the restroom to the floor.

The only thing we did differently before the second meeting with Houston was use a diamond-and-one defense, where we kept one defensive man (Shackelford) on Hayes, had three players across, and Alcindor stationed under the basket to protect it. We had never run the diamond-and-one at UCLA before that game, and we never ran it again, so I didn't have a lot of experience with it myself.

We felt that by making that defensive change, it would give our players a little something different with which to work, to try something new. Players need to be given something new every once in awhile to keep them fresh. I didn't think it was necessary—we didn't make the change with fear of playing Houston again. I felt we were going to beat the Cougars with Alcindor healthy; there was no question in my mind about that.

My assistant, Jerry Norman, suggested that when we play Houston again, we should go to a box-and-one. I told Jerry that if we go to a box-and-one, we would have to take Alcindor out of the paint. But, Jerry's suggestion is the reason that we eventually went to a diamond-and-one. We worked on the scheme for awhile before getting into the tournament because we felt, no question, that we would meet

Houston in the tournament. I still felt that we were the two best teams in the country.

The semifinal game was a good time, as our only experience with it, to change the defense. The diamond-and-one certainly worked that night against the Cougars. Hayes was held to 10 points in the game.

When the two best teams in the country are playing, like we had in the semifinals, people sometimes feel that the championship game is not as big because of the competition. I don't think that was true with us after playing Houston. I do think, however, sometimes the championship game will not be as well played as the semifinal. It may be because of the fact that teams can prepare more for the semifinal. Not knowing who they would be playing in the final, coaches have to sort of be thinking of two teams. So, in the semifinal game, you have to be more prepared. We felt, going into that 1968 semifinal game, that Houston was the best team in the country, next to us. We happened to be on the same side of the bracket or our teams would have met in the championship game. Regardless of who we played in the semifinals, we still had to win that game and the next for the championship. Our goal every year was to win our conference so we could get into the tournament and then concentrate on winning the national championship.

Down deep I didn't feel that we would have many problems in the championship game if we beat Houston. Anyone could lose a single game, but I felt that we were definitely a much better team than either of the other two semifinal teams, North Carolina or Ohio State. I thought the team that had the best chance of beating us in the Final Four was Houston, but I didn't think they could and I didn't think they would. In my opinion, we were better. I think ultimately, we didn't have any trouble with them at all. As it so happened, we met Carolina for the championship in what was an easy game for us, winning 78-55.

Part III: The '70s

CHAPTER 6

St. Louis, Missouri
March 24 & 26, 1973

At first-glance, Bill Walton, with the exception of his height, didn't look like a basketball player when he first played varsity basketball with the UCLA Bruins in the 1971-1972 season. Many people couldn't believe this lanky, red-headed, surfer-looking kid from San Diego could play college basketball. Walton quickly proved his skeptics wrong, becoming the unanimous National Player of the Year during his first two seasons, and sharing the award during his final season.

In the 1972-1973 season, Walton led the Bruins as they became the first program in NCAA history to win back-to-back undefeated national championships. By the end of the season, the Bruins also had won 75 straight games. Walton was one of the top rebounders that season, averaging 16.9 a game, and had a 20.4 points per game scoring average.

The pinnacle of Walton's season, and one of the highlights of his career, came in the 1973 title game against Memphis State (now simply known as Memphis), as he scored 44 points, including 21-for-22 from the field. The one shot he missed actually started to go in, but rolled out.

Walton, inducted into the Basketball Hall of Fame in 1993, was the number one pick in the 1974 NBA draft. He spent 13 seasons in the

1973 Final, UCLA vs. Memphis State

NBA, where he won titles with Portland and Boston. Today, Walton spends time as a motivational speaker and television analyst. He is considered to be one of the best-ever to play college basketball.

1973 All-Tournament Team

Ernie DiGregorio, Providence
Steve Downing, Indiana
Larry Finch, Memphis State
Larry Kenon, Memphis State
Bill Walton, UCLA
   (Most Outstanding Player)

Final Four Participants

Indiana
Memphis State
Providence
UCLA

National Semifinals

Memphis State 98, Providence 85
UCLA 70, Indiana 59

National Championship

UCLA 87, Memphis State 66

Bill Walton

Growing up in San Diego, UCLA was always my top choice for a college. There was no second choice. Other schools came with promises of building their program around me, and having me set scoring records, but my whole life had been about the dream of being a part of a special team. That's what UCLA was all about.

The team concept that Coach John Wooden preached and lived, made everything perfect at UCLA. Playing basketball was a privilege that you earned. It was an honor to play for the Bruins.

We expected to be in the Final Four every year. Although we didn't ever call it the Final Four ... I think that name originated when people started believing that it was OK to get that far in the tournament and lose. At UCLA, we expected to go undefeated and win every game that we ever played. When we didn't do that, it was a major, stunning disappointment. From the very beginning of the season, part of our natural, daily mindset was that we were going to win the national championship that year and every year.

Our goal was close to being realized when, with a 29-0 record, we reached the 1973 title game against Memphis State. We knew we had to play outstanding basketball against the Tigers. They were a very good team with Larry Kenon, Bill Robinson, Larry Finch, Bill Laurie, and were well coached by Gene Bartow. We were also painfully aware of how we had stunk up the gym against Florida State in 1972. More recently, we knew that we didn't take care of business in the 1973 semifinal game against Indiana, considering the Hoosiers went on a 22-0 run against us. (Actually, each team in that game went on a 22-0 run. In the first half, UCLA went on the run; and in the second half, Indiana had theirs.) We played absolutely terrible in that game. Our team knew as a collective group that we needed to bring everything that we had to the Memphis State game. We did, it worked, and it was great. Too bad we didn't have it together the next year against North Carolina State.

Although I was not the type of player who would get the ball each time down the court to go one-on-one with my defender, I was fortunate enough to hit 21-of-22 shots from the field that night, and score 44 points, an NCAA championship game record. The one shot that I missed was a short jumper from right in front of the hoop in the first half. I immediately snatched the rebound and stuck the ball right back in the basket. Coach Wooden always tells me, "Bill, I used to think you were a good player until you missed that one shot."

Our guards had 23 assists in that championship game. Greg Lee had an NCAA championship game record 14 assists, and Larry Hollyfield had a career-high nine assists. The ball was moving with exquisite crispness, a thing of beauty. The involvement of everybody on the squad was incredible. I was simply the recipient of the great passing and the precision teamwork that Coach Wooden had prepared us for all of the time.

During one of the timeouts late in the game, after I had scored numerous times in a row on virtually the same play, Greg Lee got Coach Wooden's attention and said, "Coach, can somebody else shoot besides Bill? We're winning by 25 points."

Coach Wooden looked quizzically back at Lee and said simply, "Why?"

Out of another timeout, I told Greg, "When I nod my head, throw it up there." On that possession, Greg was near midcourt when I gave him the signal. He did a double-take then threw a beautiful lob pass that I was able to go up and drop in for two points. Greg Lee was incredible.

Playing with Greg was an unbelievable honor and privilege. The single sentence that sums up Lee's capabilities and contributions the best, was when our great forward Keith Wilkes (now Jamaal) was with the Los Angeles Lakers. The Lakers had just acquired Magic Johnson, who was starting to dazzle people with his brilliant passing. Someone asked Jamaal, "What's it like playing with Magic Johnson and all of the unbelievable passes you get?"

Jamaal's answer was appropriately, "Hey, I played with Greg Lee in college."

Greg had a terrific ability to pass the ball perfectly to the receiver on time and in rhythm. There was nothing that the defense could do about it. Greg's selflessness was incredibly important to our overall success at UCLA. The flow and creativity of the offense were most often generated by Greg.

The Memphis State game was not about me as an individual, even though I get far too much individual credit for it; the game was about UCLA basketball and the dreams of John Wooden coming together. We wanted to win for Coach Wooden. I could never imagine playing for anyone in college other than him. He is a special guy and a wonderful teacher. It was simply so much fun to be a part of that unique team and era.

Coach Wooden made sure that we kept focus on our team in practice, instead of others. That philosophy made us a closer-knit group. We never focused on the other teams, so it never became easy to overlook them, even during our huge scoring margin season of 1972. We never went over the other team's plays during a shoot-around, which we never had. Coach Wooden firmly believed that it was more important to spend time preparing ourselves. He felt that players make plays; plays don't make players. His whole focus was preparing us to be great ballplayers. He began with a foundation of developing our own personal character. He shaped us in that regard before he even started to attempt to make us into quality basketball players.

Coach's philosophy is that it is so much more important to focus on the things that we can control than to waste time on the things that we can't.

He never talked about winning and losing, but rather on the way we played. Coach challenged each of us to play our perfect game, and to create an environment where it was our style of game being played. He was an unbelievable teacher in preparing us mentally, spiritually and physically. When game time came, we felt that we were invincible and could do anything we wanted.

The vast majority of us, having grown up in Southern California, had our dreams come true by being one of the chosen few that John Wooden had hand-selected to carry on his vision, his dream, about what the game of basketball should be. To be a part of that UCLA family is like nothing else anywhere in the world.

In my real family's house, we grew up without a television set. In an era when there was not a lot of basketball on TV, I distinctly remember the first game I ever saw on the tube, the 1965 championship game between UCLA and Michigan. The Wolverines had big, bruising guys like Cazzie Russell and Bill Buntin, to play UCLA's small, skinny, scrawny guys such as Gail Goodrich, Keith Erickson and Kenny Washington. Watching the teams warm up, I felt there was no way that UCLA could ever beat that Michigan team. I had followed UCLA through the newspaper and on radio, but I had never seen them in person or on television.

When I saw the incredible disparity in the physical stature of those two teams, I was convinced that Michigan would have its way with the Bruins. Then, the game started and UCLA was amazing. The Bruins had teamwork, passing, quickness, a high skill level, execution of the fundamentals and conditioning. Here were these little, skinny guys, much the way I was a scrawny 13-year-old at the time, waxing Michigan.

Goodrich scored an NCAA championship game record of 42 points that night. I told myself right then that I wanted to play like that, for UCLA and John Wooden. I was lucky because my dream of doing that came true. Not only did I get a chance to play for Coach Wooden, at UCLA, in the NCAA championship game, I got to beat Gail Goodrich's record, too.

Coach Wooden had such an incredible effect on us, not just as basketball players, but as people. He really wasn't even a coach; he was a teacher. He was as inspirational and influential a person as I have ever met in my life, more so than anyone other than my mom and dad.

I was a little concerned during my first day of practice at UCLA, however, when Coach showed us how to put our shoes and socks on. He did it in such a way that there were no wrinkles in the socks and no twists to the laces. This technique is the starting point for a player. It's another example of how he taught his players to prepare

Final Four Fast Facts

Carolina's Lennie Rosenbluth is one of only three players in Atlantic Coast Conference history to be named ACC Player of the Year, ACC Tournament MVP, NCAA Regional MVP and National Player of the Year in the same season (1957).

for every eventuality, and how important it is to take care of every little detail so that we can ensure ourselves the greatest possibility of winning ... not sometimes, but every time. The slow learner that I am, I have finally come to realize that the way a player puts his shoes and socks on is a critically important part of his basketball game. I have actually taken all of my four sons to Coach Wooden's house to have him show them how to put their shoes and socks on. There is no way to describe the technique in words except to say that you really don't want to see Coach Wooden's bare feet.

1973 Final, UCLA vs. Memphis State

For me, college was a perfect time. Coach Wooden made it so much fun. There was always an incredible sense of joy, celebration and passion. That continues to this very day with John Wooden.

He approaches life every day as if he is so lucky to be a part of this wonderful game, and can still teach people. So many people, as they go through life, develop levels of cynicism, bitterness, envy and a negative personality. There is not an ounce of any of that in Coach Wooden's life. It is a wonderful honor and privilege for me that I've had a chance to grow up with Coach Wooden.

My four years at UCLA were the happiest of my life. It was a time of perfection, accomplishment and complete satisfaction. We felt so good about what it was that we were doing, the level of happiness was exhilarating.

When I left UCLA in 1974, I became the highest paid player in the history of team sports, yet the quality of my life actually went down when I joined the NBA. That's how special things were at UCLA. Everything with the Bruin program was based on the team, and how the success of everyone as an individual was vital for the team to experience ultimate, continuous success. For me, it was never better. I have spent the rest of my life relentlessly trying to duplicate those glorious days.

CHAPTER 7

Greensboro, North Carolina
March 23 & 25, 1974

Before the NCAA realized that one radio network could, and would, pay for the exclusive rights to carry the Final Four, stations from around the country were allowed to carry the live play-by-play of games, even if a local school was not represented. That rule was fine for legendary Midwestern announcer Fred White, who broadcast seven Final Fours for WIBW radio in Topeka, Kan., between 1968 and 1975.

Most of White's Final Four experiences involved the UCLA Bruins, including the 1968 rematch between UCLA and Houston, Bill Walton's 44-point performance against Memphis State, North Carolina State knocking off the Bruins, and the 1975 Bruin title, Coach John Wooden's final game and the last in the UCLA reign.

White has made a name for himself in college basketball and Major League Baseball. He has broadcast college games nationally for CBS and ESPN, regionally for the Atlantic Coast Conference, and has been the voice of the Kansas State Wildcats. White also spent 25 years as a radio announcer with MLB's Kansas City Royals.

Currently, he works for Metro Sports, a local cable sports station in the Kansas City area, broadcasts basketball games for the University of Illinois and the Big XII Conference.

Walton was a senior on that 1974 UCLA squad. To this day he considers the loss to N.C. State, which marked the beginning to the end of UCLA's domination in the tournament, one of the most disappointing and embarrassing events in his life. Behind David Thompson's 28 points and Tom Burleson's 20, the Wolfpack chopped down Walton and company, 80-77. It was such a disappointing loss to the Bruins, that many of their players, including Walton, did not want to play in the third-place game against Kansas. With the coaxing of Wooden, the team decided to play in the consolation game. To the Bruins, however, there was no consolation to not winning the national championship.

1974 All-Tournament Team

Tom Burleson, North Carolina State
Maurice Lucas, Marquette
David Thompson, NCSU
   (Most Outstanding Player)
Monte Towe, North Carolina State
Bill Walton, UCLA

Final Four Participants

Kansas
Marquette
North Carolina State
UCLA

National Semifinals

N.C. State 80, UCLA 77 (2 OT)
Marquette 64, Kansas 51

National Championship

N.C. State 76, Marquette 64

Bill Walton

March 23, 1974, was a terrible, embarrassing day in my life. When we arrived in Greensboro, N.C., for our NCAA semifinal game against the North Carolina State Wolfpack, we were wearing shorts, t-shirts and sandals (remember, we were a Southern California team). Unfortunately, there was snow on the ground. We should have known right then that we were in trouble for the game. It was a dastardly weekend. What a disappointment.

It's always special to be playing for the national championship. We just wish that we had been more together as a team when North Carolina State beat us that day, 80-77, in the semifinals. The problems that crept into our team, the injuries – the fact that I had broken my back that season and missed a block of time – and that we did not have the team chemistry and intangibles that had made our squad so special are, unfortunately, the things that stick out in my mind from that season.

North Carolina State's David Thompson was clearly the best player we ever played against in college. I was so happy for, and proud, to see that he was recognized for his brilliance by *Sports Illustrated*, even though he got into that position at my expense. David Thompson was always a class individual, who represented the greatness of basketball, along with its beauty, grace, style and fluidity.

Coach John Wooden never felt that any of our preparation time should be wasted on the other team. In the four years that I was with Coach Wooden, I never heard him talk about an opponent with the exception of Austin Carr at Notre Dame when I was a freshman, then Thompson when I was a senior. Thompson was a powerful force. He lit us up for 28 points. Maybe Coach Wooden should have talked a little longer about Thompson.

Even though people call that game Thompson versus Walton, David versus Goliath, Tom Burleson was the big man underneath on that N.C. State team. Burleson was effective, but certainly no Thompson. To this day, anytime I see my former Boston Celtic teammates Larry Bird or Kevin McHale, they always remind me, "You lost to Tommy Burleson. How could you ever lose a game to Tommy Burleson, much less a championship game? What kind of player are you?"

When you're a UCLA Bruin, just making it to the Final Four is not what the season is about. Going undefeated and winning the championship ... that's what we lived for. After we lost to the Wolfpack, we didn't want to play Kansas in the consolation game. The consolation game. You don't play for third place, you play for first place. Thank goodness the NCAA has gotten rid of those distastefully embarrassing games.

We had a long discussion with Coach Wooden and said that as starters, we would rather have the other guys play because we wanted to give the players who had sacrificed so much to make the team so unique, a chance to actually play. Coach wanted no part of that idea, so he convinced us that we would take part in the consolation game against Kansas, begrudgingly. It was embarrassing, disgraceful and humiliating even though we won.

All three of the championship (Final Four) games in which we played during my three years of varsity eligibility at UCLA, need to be put into context. In the first championship game, 1972, we didn't play

 **Final Four Fast Facts** UCLA's Kenny Washington is the only player to score at least 25 points in the championship game (1964) and not be named to the All-Tournament team.

well but we still beat Florida State. That season we had set an NCAA record for the largest scoring margin per game (30.3) in wins in the history of college basketball. Coach Wooden always talked to us about playing against an ideal opponent, and to not be satisfied with simply the winning or losing; but rather how you play is what's so critical to measuring your success. That Florida State game, which we won 81-76, was one of only two games that season that was closer than 20 points. We didn't have the control or the domination in that game

Denny Crum, Louisville coach
– On Recruiting Walton

Bruce Walton was a football player at UCLA. A UCLA graduate from San Diego, who had helped the football program recruit Bruce, called and told me about Bruce's younger brother, Bill, who was a high school basketball player. On this guy's recommendation, I went down to watch this Bill Walton. When I came back the next morning, I went into Coach Wooden's office to start planning practice with him. He asked me if the Walton kid was a good player. I said, "I think he's the best high school player I've ever seen."

Coach Wooden got up, closed the door, and said, "Don't ever make that kind of statement where anybody can hear you. It will make you look like an idiot. Plus, San Diego has never even had a Division I player, let alone the best player you've ever seen." I told him that's how I felt about Walton because of the things he could do on the court.

Coach didn't like recruiting, so he was reluctant to go down to San Diego to watch Walton. I told him, "Even if you don't believe that this could be the best high school basketball player I've ever seen, for us to get this kid you need to come watch him play and show a little interest."

We took the 20-minute flight to San Diego during the week to see Bill play. Part of the reason Coach didn't like to go out to recruit was because with all of the attention he would receive from fans at the game, he had a difficult time concentrating on the recruit. So, we sat in the top corner of the bleachers. When we got to our seats, I just let him watch the game in peace. I didn't say anything to him.

On our way back to the airport after the game I asked Coach what he thought about Walton. Wooden said, "Well, he is pretty good, isn't he." Coach Wooden didn't like to praise individuals, he liked to talk about the team, so when he made that comment, it meant that he liked Walton a lot. Luckily for us, the feeling was mutual from Walton.

that we expected and demanded of ourselves.

In our second championship game, my junior year, we played very well and hammered Memphis State. In the third one, against North Carolina State, we didn't play well and we lost. One of the real signs of a team moving forward, and individuals moving toward greatness, is the ability to play well each and every day, on consecutive occasions. To not be able to deliver as seniors was so frustrating because we had put it all together the previous year.

When we lost our last collegiate game, things had fallen completely apart for our squad. Even though that was the most talented team we had in my three years, all of the intangibles that make a team great, had eluded us. Coach John Wooden told us everyday,"Don't ever beat yourself. Do your best so that you can consider yourself a success. If you beat yourself, or cheat yourself, it's the worst kind of defeat you'll ever suffer, and you'll never get over it."

We thought he was nuts, but at that time we were winning all of our games. The winning streak eventually reached 88 games. It wasn't until we started losing that we realized that the lessons and messages that he was teaching us couldn't be more appropriate.

He was right about beating ourselves. He was right about everything. We certainly have never gotten over that embarrassing defeat of March 23, 1974. With an 11-point lead in the second half; then with a seven-point lead and the ball in the closing minutes of the second overtime, it was a game that should have been ours. I have been kicking myself ever since. That day I was a disgrace to the sport of basketball.

Fred White

The fact that the 1974 semifinal game between UCLA and North Carolina State was played in Greensboro, N.C., meant the crowd was really behind the Wolfpack. That wasn't completely unusual in those days because it seemed like wherever UCLA played away from Los Angeles, the crowd was pulling for the other team. There was a tremendous amount of pressure for the UCLA opponents. Every UCLA game in that era was a Jack and the Beanstalk-type game, or David versus Goliath, with the Bruins playing the role of the giant.

The Bruins were so good that teams almost had to play a perfect game in order to win. There was a huge mystique about the Bruins. Playing UCLA was similar to fighting your big brother ... always wondering if you have grown up enough yet to whip him. Most of the time the answer was no, you haven't.

If there was one club that I thought could knock off UCLA, before N.C. State, it was Memphis State in the 1973 NCAA championship game. The Tigers had a great team with Ron Robinson, Bill Buford, Larry Finch, Bill Laurie and Larry Kenon. That team could run, jump and score. I really thought they had a chance to beat the Bruins. UCLA's Bill Walton put on such a great performance, hitting 21 of 22 shots from the field, that Memphis State could never get into the game. The Tigers were on their heels from the early part of the contest, and got blown out by more than 20 points. So much for my prediction.

Even though people pulled for UCLA's opponents on the road, Bruin head coach John Wooden was still very respected. Not only did the team have mystique about it, Wooden also had one about him. He had built this aura of correctness, always doing the right thing, very polite, but there was still a mystery about him. You would watch Coach and his teams and think that winning couldn't be as simple as they made it look. Yet it seemingly was. During practices he concentrated on things he wanted his teams to do, but he was always extremely respectful to the opponent.

Coach Wooden's philosophy always was to worry about his team instead of the opponent. His teams practiced their system. They didn't practice with the other team in mind. I don't recall seeing any of their practices where

Final Four Fast Facts

In 1992, Duke became the first school since UCLA to win back-to-back national titles.

much was made of the other team, scouting reports, etc.

Watching UCLA play, it was obvious that it was a precision outfit. They were so fundamentally sound. Wooden was like the professor, and the father, in that environment. When teams played the Bruins, they were playing against that legend. Psychologically, those are tough things to play against. UCLA was seemingly invincible.

However, the Bruins were starting to show some cracks in the armor in 1974. They had lost three games that year which was as many games as they had lost in the previous four seasons, combined. UCLA wasn't the invincible team it once was, but it still had a great group of players. They still had some of their mystique.

That great group of UCLA players was led by center Bill Walton, who is the best big man I have ever seen at the college level. In fact, I think he was a better player than Lew Alcindor (Kareem Abdul-Jabbar). He had the best hands and was a great passer. I have never seen a big man who understood the game as well as Walton. Two things that stunned me when I saw him for the first time were his quickness, his great hands and his passing ability. He played hard and was relentless.

The North Carolina State Wolfpack knew that they were good, with their only loss coming against UCLA earlier in the season on a neutral court in St. Louis. The Wolfpack players felt, for the most part, that they did not play well against the Bruins in that earlier game. It may have worked to their advantage that they were playing UCLA for a second time that year, by taking away some of that UCLA mystery. Therefore, there was an extra intensity on the court that day.

North Carolina State had, what I would consider, the perfect starting five to face UCLA. Tim Stoddard was a powerful, physical banger at one forward position. David Thompson, the other forward, is the closest thing I've seen to Michael Jordan in terms of leaping ability and quickness. Monte Towe was a little guy who did a good job of running the North Carolina State offense at the point. Moe Rivers was a pretty good-sized two guard. Tom Burleson was 7-4 in the middle. That was really a pretty good combination of players to make up an excellent team.

There was a little bit of a taint because North Carolina State had been on probation in the 1973 season because of the recruiting battle over Thompson. Still, that team had such great balance in their starting five.

Going into the game, people marked it as Bill Walton against David Thompson, but actually, that match-up wasn't the key to the game because of the play of people around those guys. Burleson, for instance, was a very big factor in the game. He played very well against Walton. He almost made a bucket at the end of regulation that would have won the game for them. Instead, the shot didn't fall and the game ended up going into double-overtime.

Burleson was effective against Walton. He was not the player that Walton was, but he did go on to have a pretty good career in the pros. Throughout the season he was tabbed as being "just big." He was more than "just big" though, because he could play.

Although his box score doesn't show it, Stoddard made a lot of big plays for the Wolfpack. He got some big rebounds and seemingly chased down every loose ball. Tim was a rugged, physical player, and threw himself at UCLA every chance he got. Stoddard went on to have a very good Major League Baseball career, mainly making his name with the Baltimore Orioles.

All of the Wolfpack players contributed in the semifinal game. It was a lot more than Walton vs. Thompson; it was really team against team.

There was some doubt as to whether or not Thompson could play late in the tournament. He took a nasty fall in the East Regional finals against Pittsburgh. David was a great leaper, at least as good of a leaper as Jordan. Against Pitt, Thompson was at the very top of his leap, got somersaulted and landed on his head. He received a nasty cut on his head, and was knocked out for a few minutes. There was some doubt if he was going to play in the national semifinals more than a week later. Obviously, he did play against UCLA; and he played very well.

Thompson was probably the one player on that N.C. State team with whom UCLA could not match-up. No other teams really could, either. David was certainly one of the best college players ever. He was sensational.

The Wolfpack hung close with UCLA throughout the game. Two big deficits they were able to overcome were in the second half and the second overtime. In the second half, State trailed by 11 points and was able to comeback and tie it up. With the feeling that they did not play well in the meeting between the two teams earlier that season, when the Wolfpack got behind, they still believed they could come back. That was a luxury most teams did not experience against the Bruins.

The thing I remember most was that when North Carolina State would make a comeback, they would put the ball in a deep freeze and hold it in an attempt to get one last shot to win. It didn't work for them a couple of times, in regulation and the first overtime.

State held the ball at the end of regulation trying to get the last shot. They got that last shot but missed. During the first overtime, only two points were scored by each team. Again, it

Utah's Jerry Chambers, who scored 70 points and grabbed 35 rebounds in the two 1966 Final Four games, is the only player to win the Most Outstanding Player award for the tournament while playing for the team that finished fourth in the tournament.

was North Carolina State holding the ball, trying to get in position to win it at the end of the first extra period.

The Wolfpack got behind in the second overtime by seven points, and came back to win the game in that extra period. When they got behind by seven, most people, myself included, thought they were dead. When they came back, the UCLA players had to be thinking, "Son of a gun, we've put these guys away twice, yet they still keep coming back. What do we have to do to win?" UCLA was used to the idea that once it put a team away, they stayed away. State overcame two big deficits in that semifinal game, and it was almost as if UCLA wasn't used to anybody coming back to challenge them again.

Stories From the Final Four: The '70s

The outcome of the game was based on a combination of things. UCLA wasn't playing as well as it could at the end of that season. North Carolina State was certainly one of the best teams that the Bruins had to play in that long dominant stretch of the NCAA Tournament when they had won it all. Before the N.C. State semifinal game, the Bruins had won 38 consecutive NCAA Tournament games. When the semifinal game was all over after the second overtime, the Wolfpack had won, 80-77.

A player's psyche can't be measured, obviously, but there was some speculation as to whether or not Walton was going to play in the third-place game against Kansas, and that UCLA may not play. It was almost as if the Bruins decided their season was over and done with after losing to N.C. State, so there was no reason to play. As it turned out, the two teams did play that third-place game, and Walton played quite a bit.

When those UCLA squads got on a mission, they played with such great confidence that not many teams could beat them. The 1974 team, however, was not one of those unbeatable teams. They had a little of that invincibility stripped away from them; just enough that the combination of North Carolina State playing in its backyard (Greensboro), having played UCLA once before during that season, and believing that the Bruins could be beat, were huge confidence-builders. The Wolfpack then played a heck of game to win it.

Wooden and the Bruins won their first title in Kansas City in 1964. After that, they grew college basketball into the giant that it has become. The NCAA Tournament outgrew the arenas in which they were playing. That is one of the reasons that the 1964 Final Four was the last

Final Four Fast Facts

Three No. 1 seeds (Kentucky, Michigan, North Carolina) advanced to the 1993 Final Four for the first time since seeding was introduced in 1979. The other Final Four team, Kansas was a No. 2 seed. The Jayhawks beat the other top seed, Indiana, in the regional finals.

one in Kansas City's Municipal Auditorium, which had hosted more college basketball championship games (nine) than any other place. (The 1988 tournament at Kansas City's Kemper Arena was the last one played in anything but a dome.) UCLA is the team that put college basketball totally on the map and made it bigger than it had been. UCLA became such a high-profile program that it brought the rest of college basketball up several levels.

If you look back at the history of college basketball, the Bruins came along when basketball really needed them. College basketball needed one team that could elevate the whole NCAA, and they got that team with UCLA. Then, their dominating run ended when it needed to because people started to get the feeling that nobody but UCLA could ever win. When that changed, and everybody else figured they had a chance to win, interest in the NCAA Tournament increased again.

After UCLA lost in the 1974 semifinals, some people couldn't help but wonder if the Bruins' domination was over. They came back and won the title in 1975, Wooden's last year. That was the end of their dynasty.

CHAPTER 8

Philadelphia, Pennsylvania
March 27 & 29, 1976

Indiana University entered the 1976 NCAA Final Four on a mission. This was supposed to be the year they battled for a second straight national championship. Undefeated and ranked number one entering the tournament in 1975, they were defeated in the Mideast Regional final by Kentucky, despite 33 points and 22 rebounds from first team All-American center Kent Benson. Scott May, also a first team All-American, and the team's leading scorer, had suffered a broken wrist late in the season and was a surprise starter in the contest. He managed only two points and the Hoosiers saw their undefeated season and title hopes fall to a team they had defeated soundly earlier in the year.

The Hoosiers 1975-1976 season record stood at 30-0 entering the final weekend of the season and there were two games to play before they could feel the season had been a success. Their first opponent in the Final Four was the UCLA Bruins, a team the Hoosiers had defeated earlier in the season. Legendary UCLA coach John Wooden (an Indiana native who grew up 20 miles from the Indiana University campus) was gone and Indiana coach Bob Knight would soon be taking a major step toward becoming a coaching legend in his own right. Kent Benson remembers the weekend well.

All five starters of Indiana's undefeated 1976 national championship team went on to play in the NBA. Quinn Buckner, Bobby Wilkerson and Scott May were first-round draft picks in 1976, while Tom Abernethy was selected in the third round of the same year. Kent was selected as the number-one draft pick in 1977 by the Milwaukee Bucks, where he joined former teammate Buckner.

Benson and May returned to Bloomington, Ind., after their basketball careers were completed. Kent owns All-American Estate Planning, specializing in advanced tax planning. Scott owns and operates a property development company. Wilkerson and Abernethy live in the Indianapolis area where Bobby works with inner-city youth, and Tom owns an indoor sports facility called the Indiana Basketball Academy. After a stint as the Dallas Mavericks head coach, Quinn is a frequent visitor to the Hoosier state where he does television broadcasts for the

Indiana Pacers. Buckner's son enrolled at Indiana University and is serving as a basketball manager under Bob Knight.

Kent and former teammate John Laskowski have daughters playing basketball together for Bloomington North High School. The roots of this team will never stray far from home.

Editor's Note: Brad Winters, a manager for the 1976 Indiana team, wrote this introduction for Kent Benson's story.

1976 All-Tournament Team	Final Four Participants
Tom Abernethy, Indiana	Indiana
Kent Benson, Indiana	Michigan
(Most Outstanding Player)	Rutgers
Rickey Green, Michigan	UCLA
Marques Johnson, UCLA	
Scott May, Indiana	

National Semifinals	National Championship
Michigan 86, Rutgers 70	Indiana 86, Michigan 68
Indiana 65, UCLA 51	

Kent Benson

We went into the opening game of the 1976 NCAA Final Four with UCLA taking the same approach that we had taken all season long ... that we had to play to our potential. We weren't necessarily playing UCLA, as much as we were striving to reach our full potential both offensively and defensively. If we did the things that we were capable of doing, to the best of our abilities, then we would win the basketball game. And we knew that.

Throughout my entire career at Indiana we had the best group of players that we could have. We all knew our roles and we all worked hard in every practice and every game. Although we did not all run in the same crowd away from the court, we all had the greatest respect for each other, and we had a strong unity on the court. There was never disrespect for each other on, or off, the court. It was a unique situation. Each player, from the starters to the reserves, performed their best each time we hit the court.

Stories From the Final Four: The '70s

UCLA had a great team, along with a new head coach, Gene Bartow, who was taking over for the legendary John Wooden, who had retired after the 1975 season. The Bruins had great players in Richard Washington and Marques Johnson (later a teammate of mine with the NBA's Milwaukee Bucks). I remember Coach Knight started me out on Washington, who was very quick and was keeping me out on top. So Coach put Tom Abernethy on Washington. Abernethy and Bobby Wilkerson were our two best defenders. The game seemed to change after that switch.

In 1966, net income from the tournament exceeded $500,000 for the first time. As the tournament enters 2000, the net income is approaching the $10-million mark.

We all fell into our roles on both ends of the court and set the pace for the game. I do not remember a lot of particulars of the game. We had a job to do and we were able to take another step toward our final goal. I realize the significance of the game more now, with the dominance of UCLA ending, than I did at the time. By the time we arrived in our locker room after the game, we had already forgotten about the Bruins and were preparing mentally for Michigan, our opponent in the national championship game.

That is how the whole season went for our ballclub. It did not matter who we played, the mission was always to play to our potential and to not play the opponent's game. We did not take UCLA or any of the other teams lightly. We just knew that our opponent was ourselves and that we had a goal to reach in every game, and for the season. We had our eyes on the national championship from the final game in 1975, until the final game in 1976. Once we got on the court, it didn't matter who we were facing, we just knew what we had to do to win. It was within ourselves.

The thing I remember most as the championship game against Michigan started, was when Wilkerson was knocked out after being accidentally elbowed by Wayman Britt. He was unconscious and he seemed to lie there for so long. We did not play well for the rest of the first half because we were worried about his condition.

When we entered the locker room at halftime, Coach Knight knew that we were all concerned about Bobby. Coach assured us that he was all right and that he was resting at the hospital. He would be kept there for observation. Coach knew that was our foremost concern. Once we knew that Bobby was going to be all right, we were able to go out in the second half and make it an entirely different ballgame. We went into the locker room trailing by eight points, and were able to come out and win the game, 86-68.

In the closing moments of the game, Coach Knight took each player out of the game, one at a time. I still remember Quinn Buckner doing a dance on the floor, knowing that we had finally reached our goal. I hugged Scott May after I came out of the game. A picture of that ran in *Sports Illustrated*. I looked up in the stands at my mom and dad, and my family. There was a great sense of relief but I also thought, "Well, now we've done it, what's next?"

There were some tough games for us through the 1975-1976 season, but we never gave up and we never thought about losing. We knew that whatever situation we were in, we were going to end up winning. It's hard to explain, except to say that this was a special team. Something that started in 1975 had come full circle. The commitment that we had made to each other in the locker room in Dayton, Ohio, after the loss to Kentucky in the regional final had finally brought the result for which we had been striving. There was as much relief as there was joy. All the differences in personalities, lifestyles and talents had come together collectively, and now we were NCAA national champions.

We had a common goal. Coach had always talked about playing with poise and potential. That season, for 32 games, we were able to do that. When one person was off their game, another person would pick theirs up. There was never internal criticism or turmoil. We played hard, practiced hard, and had high intensity at practices, but we had a respect for each other that was unequaled.

As I walked off the court for the final time in the 1976 season, I thanked God for the opportunity that He had given me. We had finished 32-0, a perfect season. A day has not gone by over the last 23 years, that someone has not come up to me with something to share about the championship. The championship means more to me now than it ever has, and I get to relive it every day of my life through my own memories, or through a story that someone shares. It sometimes seems like it was just yesterday.

CHAPTER 9

St. Louis, Missouri
March 25 & 27, 1978

As a junior in 1978, Jim Spanarkel was the leader on the court for the Duke Blue Devils. In the main five, besides Spanarkel, there was a redshirt junior, two sophomores and two freshmen. (That totals six, but the redshirt junior and one of the sophomores split time at the point guard position.) Needless to say, this was a team that was not expected to do much throughout the season.

On the other side, the Kentucky Wildcats were a veteran team with the exception of sophomore point guard Kyle Macy, a transfer from Purdue. The Wildcats had lost in the 1977 regional finals to eventual runner-up North Carolina. They felt they should have been the team playing for the national championship. Instead, the senior-laden team set its sights on the 1978 title ... nothing else would do.

Led by Jack "Goose" Givens' 41-point performance, the Wildcats reached their goal by defeating the Blue Devils in the championship, 94-88. Sixteen of Givens' 41 points were the final points scored for Kentucky at the end of the first half.

For the past 15 years, Spanarkel has been with Merrill Lynch in the Primus, N.J., office. His "hobby" is broadcasting where he fills in for Bill Raftery with the New Jersey Nets, along with Big East Conference games with ESPN Regional and NCAA Tournament games for CBS Sports.

Macy currently is the head coach at Morehead State University in Kentucky. Before that he spent time as an analyst for Kentucky Wildcat games with Ralph Hacker on the Kentucky Radio Network.

1978 All-Tournament Team

Ron Brewer, Arkansas
Jack Givens, Kentucky
    (Most Outstanding Player)
Mike Gminski, Duke
Rick Robey, Kentucky
Jim Spanarkel, Duke

Final Four Participants

Arkansas
Duke
Kentucky
Notre Dame

National Semifinals

Kentucky 64, Arkansas 59
Duke 90, Notre Dame 86

National Championship

Kentucky 94, Duke 88

Jim Spanarkel

Whenever anybody asks me about the 1978 title game with Kentucky, the first thing that I always think about is our team, in general, and that unbelievable season. We were a relatively young team. As a junior in 1978, I was the captain of that squad (and the captain during my senior year). So, in most people's eyes, I would probably be considered the leader of the team. As for the other starters, there were two freshmen (Gene Banks and Kenny Dennard) and a sophomore (Mike Gminski). We had another junior (John Harrell) and a sophomore (Bob Bender, who transferred from Indiana) splitting time at the point guard position.

Up until that 1978 season, we hadn't had successful college careers in the win-loss column. Duke basketball actually went through a period of time from the late 1960s to 1977 where the program was down. In fact, not only did the program not make it to the NCAA Tournament between 1966 and 1978, but in the previous four seasons before the run in 1978, the team had been last in the Atlantic Coast Conference. During my first year in the league, we were last. In my second season we were last again, but we turned the corner by starting to play more competitively. Then, our team finished second in the league behind North Carolina during that 1978 season. With that turnaround, our coach, Bill Foster, was named the ACC Coach of the Year.

Coming into the 1977-78 season, the team was not expected to do as well as it did. We became somewhat of a Cinderella story. We were young and awkward at the beginning of the season, but about halfway through the year, we started to click. After losing our last regular season game to North Carolina, we caught fire winning the next seven games through the ACC and NCAA Tournaments. Our team peaked at the perfect time of the year. Was Duke picked to do that well? No, which is why the country, in general, grasped onto us as the Cinderella team and the young, upstart team trying to go after the big boys.

The way in which the NCAA Tournament started for us, it appeared as though fate may have been on our side. In fact, we probably should have lost our opening game, against Rhode Island, at the end, with their team having three or four opportunities in the last seven seconds under their own basket to put the ball in for the win. They couldn't find the hole, so we dodged the losing bullet in the first-round with a 63-62 win. Things didn't get much easier in the second-round with Pennsylvania. That was a tough game, but they made some mistakes down the stretch, then we capitalized for the win, 84-80.

Villanova was our next opponent, in the East Regional finals. Before that game, some of the Villanova people were saying that Duke was just a big, plodding team. They tested us with some of those blackboard comments. Funny, that game turned out to be our easiest in the tournament, as we beat the Wildcats by 18 points. We were going to the Final Four!

Despite the fact that we were on a roll and were a young, carefree team, I would probably be lying if I said we didn't feel any pressure heading into the Final Four, and our semifinal game with Notre Dame. We definitely had butterflies in our stomachs. We had reached the pinnacle of college basketball for that one year, with a team that just clicked for some reason. Our team got along. We didn't worry about things, we simply went after teams, played hard, and played well together.

We didn't get hung up on what we were accomplishing that year, which is the beauty of that season. If anyone on this team was asked what the key was to our season, they would say that things just happened for us that year. None of us really know exactly why we were successful that season; we just were. The season and our success evolved, especially from the fact that we were so young, and nobody expected us to do well, to the last six weeks where we clicked and played great basketball.

Basically, we had a team full of guys who were good competitors. Dennard and Banks, as forwards, for instance, worked hard and were great guys to have on a team. The other players knew that if we were diving for a loose ball, at least one of those two guys was going to be diving after it, also. Looking back, there isn't really a finite instance or turning point in that season. We got on a roll, and nobody on the team asked why it was happening, we just ran with it.

Notre Dame, which we played in the national semifinals, had a very good team that year, with several guys on their roster who later turned out to be pro players, like Kelly Tripucka, Orlando Woolridge and Bill Laimbeer. (Although the Blue Devils had five from that team who later played pro, including myself, Gminski, Banks, Dennard and Bobby Bender, who is the head coach at the University of Washington.) That was a tough game against the Irish, but we pulled out the 90-86 win to earn a meeting in the championship game with the Kentucky Wildcats.

Kentucky came into the game as the team that had been predicted to finish No. 1 in the country. Therefore, I think they were somewhat mechanical in their approach to the title game. Since the Wildcats were expected from the start of the season to be there, and they were there, their team maybe took a little different approach than we did. They came into the game on a mission, and almost appeared robotic in the way they were doing things. We were just a bunch of young guys, the upstart, having a great time.

The Wildcats were led by Rick Robey and Mike Phillips on the front line. They also featured Jack "Goose" Givens, who had a career night against us; one of those games where he just couldn't miss. He finished the game shooting 18-27 (.667) from the field, including Kentucky's final 16 points of the first half. One of his baskets, in particular, from that first half scoring stretch, sticks out to me. (We played a match-up zone defense and I was in the middle of the floor, so I could see all of this clearly.) Givens took a corner jump shot, and as the ball was on its way, it was obvious that the ball was going to hit the side of the backboard. Anticipating the ricochet, I started to glide toward the middle of the lane to be in better position for the rebound. Instead of ricocheting, the ball just grazed the side of the backboard and went through the basket. Givens actually banked one of his shots off the corner of the backboard facing the sideline, for two points! We were about 18 minutes into the game then ... I knew we were in for a long night if he was going to be hitting shots like that.

The Wildcat front line set the tone for their team, and that's the type of game we had in the championship, with a lot of banging inside. They went up on us with five minutes left in the game, but we made one last run. That run forced Kentucky to bring its starters back in the game to put us away, and put the final touches on the championship, 94-88. Kentucky had the better team that year, but for about 30 of the 40 minutes, it was a pretty good game.

The hot hand of the Wildcats' "Goose" Givens led all scorers with 41 points. Banks led the Blue Devils with 22 points, I had 21, and Gminski totaled 20. Each of us had also scored at least 20 points in the Notre Dame game, making us the only threesome to each score at least 20 points in both of the Final Four games. That's a nice distinction, although it's not one of those things I'm going to have printed on my shirt sleeve. The funny thing about having that kind of dubious honor is that when I go into New York each day from New Jersey, they're still going to charge me four dollars to cross the bridge.

Even though the NCAA championship game was the best game in which a college player could play, our team had a blast simply reaching the finals. What sticks in my mind about the final game with Kentucky, in particular, is losing after such a hard-fought battle. Having gone all the way to that particular point, and the disappointment of not actually winning the whole thing, really stuck in the minds of everybody involved, from the players and coaches to the fans and university's people.

Just like most things in today's society, when we are going through an experience, we don't "stop and smell the roses" enough. Especially now, we're so busy with our lives that we don't take the time to really appreciate what we're doing and what we have. That was the case in 1978. Do 20-year-old kids, give or take a couple years, know how good they have it? They probably don't. We happened to be playing NCAA basketball for a national championship, and I guarantee that none of us knew how good we had it.

Playing in the Final Four was an experience in which I may not remember all the details, because all of the little details are kind of blurred together in my mind, but the fact that I was there and was a part of it, and that we had some fun along the way as we damn near won the tournament, is unforgettable. The dynamics of our team really left me with the mentality that if people get on the same page, and nobody is worrying about personal numbers, everything else will take care of itself. One of the interesting things with that Duke team is that because we were not successful prior to 1978, even though Banks and Dennard were heralded freshmen, nobody on the team went through that season saying, "If we win and I score my 20 points, I'm going to get a lot of recognition." None of the guys, at that point in our lives, were thinking that way. If we were honestly looking at the next year, maybe some of us would have wound up with the hysteria that came with finishing our season in the NCAA championship game.

With everyone returning from our Cinderella team, Duke went into the 1979 season as the No. 1 team in the nation. We got off to a good start, winning our first six games of the year. At the end of December we played in the ECAC Holiday Tournament in New York against Ohio

State and St. John's. We were up by double-digits in each of those games with about 15 minutes left, and lost both of them. Throughout the rest of the season, we never really regrouped from that tournament. We never got our starch back. We played OK that year, but never lived up to the potential that we had coming into the season.

During the first round of the NCAA Tournament, Duke (No. 2 seed) and North Carolina (No. 1 seed) were placed in the East Region, playing our games in Raleigh. In the opening round, we played St. John's, while the Tar Heels started with Pennsylvania. Both ACC teams ended up losing their Sunday afternoon games. For us it came crashing down against a team that had beaten us a couple months earlier. Carolina lost to Penn, 72-71. The headline in the paper the next day was, "Black Sunday" because we were both local teams, ranked in the top 10, expected to do well in the tournament, but both lost in the first round. Sure, there was probably some hysteria around our team that year.

Lew Alcindor is the only player to have been named the Most Outstanding Player of the Final Four three times (1967, 1968, 1969).

In 1978 that simply was not the case. None of us was worrying about who was getting paper clippings. We were worrying about whether or not we were going to win. Taking that attitude from the experience has really helped me see the light in a lot of different aspects of my life. I have children now with whom I'm very involved. I help on a real peripheral side of coaching, but I can look at that team and try to base all of the things I pass along to them, whether it's in basketball or not, in terms of the attitude. Our 1978 Duke team had an attitude of trying to stand out, not stick out. We realized there's a major difference between the two.

Kyle Macy

When you consider dominant teams through the years, the 1978 University of Kentucky basketball team should be mentioned.

I'm a little biased, obviously, but I think if the media coverage had been the same as it has been since 1979, we would have received a lot more attention as being one of the most dominant teams through the years. I have even heard that whichever network covered the Final Four that year, had technical problems with the film, which is why there isn't a lot of footage from our championship game. There were big Final Four crowds in the late 1970s, but it wasn't the event that it is now.

The 1978 Kentucky basketball team, finished the season with a 30-2 record and won the national championship tournament. The two games we lost that year were both on the road. One was an overtime game where three of our starters had fouled out, and the other we were just worn down from possibly practicing too hard.

Our front line was big, strong and agile. Our perimeter players were excellent shooters with Jack "Goose" Givens, Truman Claytor, Jay Shidler and myself, that had the three-point shot been around, we would have out scored our opponents by an even greater margin. We played good man-to-man and zone defense. We could play a fast-breaking game or a walk-up style. We could overpower teams or we could finesse them. We could beat teams in any way needed. There just wasn't a weak spot on our squad.

That 1978 season was an exciting one for all of us. This Kentucky team was a group of seniors that had a lot of success but had not gotten over the hump. As freshmen in 1975, they lost in the championship game in San Diego to John Wooden's last UCLA team. As sophomores they won the NIT with Rick Robey out with a bad knee. As juniors they made it to the NCAA East Regionals before North Carolina knocked them out. They had gotten close in each of their first three years, but never really reached their goal.

I signed with Purdue out of high school. Kentucky was originally one of my final three choices. But because I was late deciding, the Kentucky coaches pushed me to make a decision so they could finish their recruiting. I told them that if they needed to go ahead and sign someone, then my answer was no because I wasn't ready to commit. The guard they signed instead of me was Truman Claytor, who was my backcourt mate when I joined the Wildcats.

Later when I contacted Kentucky to let the coaches know that I wanted to transfer, Coach Hall discouraged me from making the move even though he knew there would be a senior at the point guard position the year I had to sit out. That meant I could slide right into that guard spot. Up to that point they hadn't taken many transfers. Luckily, I talked them into taking me. As suspected, sitting out that year was difficult, even though I practiced every day with the team, got to watch films and do all those things to be ready to play.

It wasn't like I was thrown directly into the fire, but it probably took me about four or five games into the 1977-1978 season before I started to feel comfortable running the offense. Once I relaxed and got a little bit more comfortable and confident out there playing games, things started to mesh together. I think the big guys, the front line, our seniors, were kind of looking for some leadership out on the floor, which is generally the responsibility of the point guard. I wasn't a real vocal leader at the point, but my style helped us maintain composure and control the pace and tempo of the game.

As a sophomore first-year player, guys like Mike Phillips, James Lee and Rick Robey made my job pretty easy. Robey and Phillips set great picks to help get shots off, but they also were so physical down low, it really opened up the outside. It wasn't like I felt the need to do too much. The opposite was true ... I tried to let the game come to me and read what our guys were doing.

This team was always very focused. On our first day of conditioning in the fall of 1977, instead of talking about teamwork and what we needed to do to win, we were talking about what we needed to do to win the national championship. Our mindset was not just to have a good year, it was to win the whole tournament. A lot of that mentality came from the fact that we were being led by four seniors.

When we did reach the Final Four. we were really excited to be there, but we weren't there just to be happy. Because of the close-but-not-quite success the seniors had in previous years, we weren't just playing that season to make the Final Four. Our goal was to win the national championship. Whereas some teams feel that once they reach the Final Four, everything else is gravy, we were there to win everything. Head Coach Joe B. Hall really stressed that we shouldn't celebrate until we won it all.

Coach Hall was masterful at getting us ready for games, especially the Final Four. He made it a point in one of our early practices preparing for the semifinals to stress the circus atmosphere of a Final Four. There are a lot of distractions in which we could get caught up, but we had to be focused on accomplishing our goal. The guys had gotten close to the prize, but we wanted to wrap it up this time.

Kentucky's toughest game of the Final Four was the Arkansas semifinal with their triplets of Sidney Moncrief, Ron Brewer and Marvin Delph. It was nip and tuck toward the end when we got a fast break run out against their press. I threw the ball over the top to Jack Givens. His basket put us up by six points and finally put the nail in the coffin with under a minute to play. That was our toughest of the two games.

After that semifinal match with Arkansas, Coach Hall wanted to go out and take the team to dinner. Instead, Robey asked if we could go back to the hotel and watch films of the other semifinal game between Duke and Notre Dame to prepare for the Monday night championship against the Blue Devils. You could tell that this was a senior-oriented ball club, in that we were focused on what we were doing.

Coach's preparation really began with our preseason conditioning program, too. Joe B. was an innovator in team conditioning. Most teams at that time weren't into a lot of preseason conditioning. (Nowadays, basically every basketball team lifts weights and has a preseason running program.) I now realize that not only was the physical aspect of working out important, but the mental toughness it develops is especially key. That's why I think that if you reach a Final Four, with all the pressure of a close game or the huge number of people watching, you're mentally tough enough to handle it based on that preseason conditioning. That mentality helps with the difficult preparation during the week, you don't want to go out on the court and embarrass yourself.

Hall's players knew, or at least I always felt, that nothing was going to happen on the court that we wouldn't have been prepared for, from what we did in our practice sessions, the film breakdown, and everything else we did during the course of a week leading up to a game. Once the game started, we didn't really need to pay that much attention to the bench because Coach had us so prepared that we even knew what to do if our opponents made some type of switch against us.

Final Four® Fast Facts

1973 was the first year that the NCAA used the Saturday afternoon, Monday evening format for the Final Four.

There has been some talk over the years about how guys couldn't play for Coach Hall because they felt like every time they made a mistake, they would have to look over at the bench or feared being taken out of the game. I never had that problem. He just prepared us so much that we felt comfortable knowing what was going to happen, so we could just go out there and play. Coach might go on his tirades on the sidelines with officials, or whatever, but that shouldn't affect the players because they were so prepared and focused on what was needed on the court.

His discipline was very important to our squad. He stressed that basketball is a team game and everybody needed to rely on each other to reach that team goal. The more time that passes since he retired, the more that people appreciate what he accomplished as the head coach.

Because the title was our season-long focus, a lot of people looked at our approach to the game and winning in the wrong way, saying, when we won games, that we weren't enjoying ourselves. Our attitude and the idea that we weren't having fun really got blown out of proportion after our semifinal game.

We played the second game of the semifinals; a late, hard-fought game. The Final Four press conference was early the next morning. The three or four of us who went to that press conference were still half-asleep from the night before, so we weren't joking around like the Duke freshmen. We were kind of in a daze. It takes awhile to unwind after a tough game, then to get up early the next morning for a press conference, made things more difficult. Because of that, the media saw this young, happy-go-lucky squad (Duke) just out having a bunch of fun going up against this older squad who didn't enjoy basketball. Blah, blah, blah.

I guess it's a compliment to say we looked business-like, or robotic, which has been suggested over the years. Our older guys realized that an opportunity to win the tournament doesn't come along very often, whereas the Duke players may have felt that they were going to be there for the next four years. The entire season for that Kentucky team was simply a situation of our guys knowing what we wanted to do.

Again, we were a dominant team. No matter what opponents tried to do, with the exception of those two losses, we could adjust our style of play and get a lead ... then they were in trouble. That may have been one of the reasons people didn't think we were having fun, because we played with a lot of confidence out there knowing what we had to do, then went about our business so we could get to where we wanted to go – the championship. Regardless of how people labeled us at the time, we've celebrated ever since that final game.

In the championship game, Duke came out in a 2-3 zone defense. Givens started hitting some shots from the corner or flashing in the middle for the easy shot. He made life pretty simple for me. All year long whenever he got the hot hand, I just tried to find him on the floor. Duke never really made an adjustment to stop him. When the Blue Devils tried to step up, Goose was quick enough to give their defense a ball fake and go by Mike Gminski and the rest of their front line players. Givens had an unbelievable night.

UCLA's Bill Walton has the record for most points in the finals with 44, but in retrospect Jack easily could have broken that had he stayed in the whole game. We got a big lead and Coach Hall took the main guys out. The reserves squandered the lead to get to the final score but had Goose not sat out for those minutes, I'm sure he could have scored in the high 40s if he wanted to. Instead, he finished the game with 41 points. Givens had nearly half of our team's points, as we defeated Duke for the national title, 94-88.

As a college coach now, a lot of things we did at Kentucky, I now use at Morehead State. Our conditioning program is similar – again, to stress the physical and mental toughness. The team concept, or attitude, is similar whereas our guys realize that we don't have star players. Even though there may be players with better abilities that we will try to use, this is a team game and everybody has to make some sacrifices for the benefit of the team. If a player isn't willing to do that, the team is never going to reach its full potential and play its best. Day to day my program now always does something that reflects back to my playing days

Without a doubt the most memorable and enjoyable time of my basketball career is winning that national title, because the NCAA Final Four Championship is what college basketball is all about. The game is not about individual accomplishments or recognition, but rather it is a team game. When your team comes together and plays as our 1978 Wildcat team did, not just in the Final Four but pretty much the whole year, it is an experience that you cherish your whole life.

CHAPTER 10

Salt Lake City, Utah
March 24 & 26, 1979

Earvin "Magic" Johnson. Larry Bird. The rivalry begins. Enough said? Probably so, but the 1979 championship game between Johnson's Michigan State Spartans and Bird's Indiana State Sycamores was an intriguing match-up for reasons other than Magic and the Legend.

Indiana State had never reached the Final Four prior to the 1978-1979 season. But this was not an ordinary season. In fact, the *1999-2000 Indiana State Media Guide* lists 1979 as "A Dream Season." For a lot of teams, a trip to the Final Four might constitute a dream season, but for this program it truly was an unreal experience, on the wings of Larry Bird. The standout from French Lick, Ind., was the NCAA Player of the Year with a 28.6 points per game scoring average (second in the NCAA that season).

The Spartans had been to the Final Four, although not since 1957. They especially couldn't believe a team this young could reach that plateau, with only one senior, two juniors and three sophomores. One of the pilots on that team was senior Greg (now Gregory) Kelser; the other was sophomore Johnson. Kelser led by example, leading the Spartans in both scoring (18.8 ppg) and rebounding (8.7 rpg).

In the highest-rated college basketball game ever televised, the Spartans knocked off the undefeated Sycamores, 75-64. Many people point to this game as the one that brought college basketball up toward the level of popularity where it is today.

Kelser was a first-round draft pick by Detroit in the 1979 draft (fourth player overall). During his NBA career, he played with Detroit, Seattle, San Diego and Indiana. For the past 15 seasons, Kelser has been broadcasting Pistons games for Fox Sports Net in Detroit as well as broadcasting for ESPN Regional and CBS Sports during the NCAA tournament.

89

1979 All-Tournament Team	**Final Four Participants**
Mark Aguirre, DePaul	DePaul
Larry Bird, Indiana State	Indiana State
Gary Garland, DePaul	Michigan State
Earvin Johnson, Michigan State	Pennsylvania
(Most Outstanding Player)	
Greg Kelser, Michigan State	
National Semifinals	**National Championship**
Michigan State 101, Pennsylvania 67	MSU 75, ISU 64
Indiana State 76, DePaul 74	

Gregory Kelser

Our Michigan State team was ranked No. 1 in the country after eight games of the 1978-1979 season, with a record of 7-1. At that point, we started playing tentative basketball; not the way we had been playing. We were fortunate to win our first two Big Ten games. In the second one we were down to Minnesota by 13, but came back and won. Then we had to go on the road and ran into an Illinois team that was 15-0 overall and ranked No. 3 in the country. They beat us by two points on an Eddie Jordan shot with three seconds to go. Two days later we traveled to Purdue, and lost at the buzzer when Arnette Holman hit a turn-around prayer from about 18 feet away. We won our next two games at home before going back on the road. In that next road game, we lost at Michigan on a free throw after the buzzer from a foul call right at the horn. The Michigan player went to the free-throw line and made one of the two for a one-point victory.

Then we went to Northwestern. Keep in mind, Northwestern hadn't won a single conference game. I don't even know if they had won any non-conference games. It wasn't a good team, but on this night it was good enough. They beat us by 18 points. Some consider that loss to be one of the biggest upsets in NCAA history, probably because two weeks before we were the No. 1 team in the country, and Northwestern was far from that distinction. But, looking at the way we were playing at that time, it wasn't that much of an upset. Northwestern caught us on one of those days when it was red hot, doing everything right, and we were doing absolutely nothing right ... the result is proof. It was just one of those games. Northwestern had a tendency for knocking off at least one big team every year. A year or two before they beat us, they upset Michigan when the Wolverines were ranked No. 1, so they were capable of shocking people. They caught us at the right time. That was pretty much when our team hit rock bottom.

At that point, we knew we had reached the absolute abyss, but looking back it was obviously the best thing that could have happened to us, because we had a very serious team meeting after that game and sort of rededicated ourselves. This wasn't the typical rock-bottom-type team meeting – it was a very good one. The meeting was productive because we all looked at ourselves and took the blame, rather than point fingers at each other and the coaches. Everybody vowed to give a little bit more, and also try to have more fun and play more loose. At that point, we really had nothing to lose. We were in sixth place in the Big Ten Conference, four games out of first place. Ohio State was 8-0 and undefeated. We were 4-4, and decided to see if we could run the table. We felt like we were fully capable.

Obviously, to prove we were capable of being the best, we had to beat the best – Ohio State. As was the case with a lot of games that season, sophomore Earvin "Magic" Johnson was a key for us in the Buckeye game. He twisted his ankle in the first half and looked like he was not going to be able to play in the second half, but he limped out there and pretty much, on one leg, helped us win that game in overtime. He had a tremendous second half and helped us get through a game which was, at that time, the most important game and one we had to win. We were truly aware that if we lost any more games we were not going to the NCAA Tournament. It was not like it is now where they take five or six teams out of the conference. Back then you either finished first, or tied for first, or you didn't go. Our work was cut out for us with the Buckeyes. Earvin realized that, so, he got himself off the trainer's table and came out there to help us win that game, even though he was hobbling. He sat out most of our next game because his ankle was so bad. That was definitely memorable.

Our team had an interesting make up. I was the only senior on the team, as well as one of the co-captains. We had junior Ron Charles, who became our sixth man after that Northwestern game. Terry Donnelly, a starting guard, was a junior. Johnson, Jay Vincent and Michael Brkovich were all sophomores. Vincent was a very gifted 6-8 wing man who could do everything. He was somewhat underestimated because he played in the same city as Earvin during high school, but take nothing away from Jay; he was an absolutely amazing basketball player.

Johnson was the other co-captain on that team. He was probably the more boisterous captain; whereas I led by example. I wasn't really big on getting in the guys' faces. Coach Jud Heathcote did that enough, that it wasn't necessary for me to do it, too. I think Earvin and I also were the hardest workers on the team which was hopefully a tremendous example for everybody else. We were the two more talented players but we were also the two hardest workers and that certainly encourages everyone else to work hard.

From the sidelines, we were led by Coach Heathcote. He is the best coach I've ever had and I've had some good ones. His knowledge of the game and his game preparation is unsurpassed. He is a tremendously hard worker, so he set the tone for everybody else. He's a perfectionist and sometimes he could be very difficult to play for because of that. He didn't find too many positives in our day-to-day performance. The coach is the type of guy who could look at a 20-point blowout and find 10 things that we did wrong, and that is what he is going to emphasize and how he's going to coach when we go to practice the next time.

Coach Heathcote never wanted us to be satisfied, which I understood after I matured a little bit more. He always felt we could do more, be better and improve. I give him a lot of credit for helping me develop my game because he spent a lot of time working with me after practice on my shot, and some of the other things that I needed to do in order to be effective in his philosophy. Whatever success I was able to achieve at the college level, I owe a ton of gratitude to Jud Heathcote.

Heading into that season, we had set our goals high because we had narrowly missed the Final Four in 1978, losing to Kentucky by three points in the regional finals. Once we finally got out of the Big Ten schedule in 1979, we felt there were no non-conference teams that would be able to handle us because they didn't know much about us, and because of our size. We had four guys at 6-8, with long arms who were good ball handlers and good scorers. That, in and of itself, was a very tough ordeal for any team to match up against.

When we got into the tournament, one of our team goals was to get an early lead and try not to let any of the games be close. All of the close games in which we were involved during the regular season, resulted in a loss and it wasn't because we didn't know how to play tight games. We just didn't have the ball and lost at the buzzer. With that in mind, we wanted to have big wins in all of our tournament games. We were able to accomplish that goal. We beat Lamar in the first game by almost 30 points; No. 8 LSU by 16 points; Notre Dame by 12 points; and Pennsylvania by 34 points.

The two teams that we ultimately wanted to play were Notre Dame and Indiana State. We ended up facing both of them. Notre Dame was a target because it was in our region, and it had so many great players. We saw them seemingly every week on television, and felt like we were just as good as they were but weren't getting nearly the coverage. We really relished the opportunity to play those guys. We got our chance at the Irish in the Mideast Regional finals.

To show the genius of Jud Heathcote, he noticed that Notre Dame never put anybody back in the defensive area on the opening tipoff. All year long we would always tip back into our defensive area to get possession, then walk the ball up the floor and run our offense. Jud added a play the day before the game with the Irish which called for me to tip the ball forward and exploit their absence in the front court. It was imperative that I win the jump ball against Orlando Woolridge; tip

During the regular 1974 season, Notre Dame ended UCLA's 88-game winning streak with a final of 71-70. N.C. State ended the Bruins' consecutive national championships at seven years.

the ball to Earvin, who would then flick it to one of our guys, who would be streaking to the basket to try to get a quick opening lead. Ideally, the streaking player was going to be Mike Brkovich. The day before the game, I told Mike to make sure he dunked it, "to make an opening statement." Our team worked on that play, called "Go."

As the play unfolded, I won the tip, tipped it to Earvin, who was right there in position in front of me, and he just redirected the ball by tapping it over his head, without catching it, to Brkovich who caught it in stride, and slammed it. Two seconds into the game, and we were up, 2-0, on a dunk. You hate to say that one simple little basket at the beginning of the game wins the game for you, but I certainly think that it was quite a start for us against the Irish.

Everything seemed to be going right for us in that ballgame. By the time the Mideast Regional final was all over, we had won 80-68. For me, besides the fact that we won, it was a terrific game. I ended the night with 34 points and 13 rebounds. Needless to say, I was ready to go that day. We all were.

Then, of course, there was Indiana State, the team that was ranked No. 1 in the country; the team that was undefeated; the team with Larry Bird, the National Player of the Year. We wanted a shot at them and we got it in the championship game.

It's interesting that many times a team going through a tournament tries to look and chart the easiest path to the title. Our bunch was unusual in that regard because we wanted to play the toughest teams. We wanted to play the teams that were the most heralded, and in doing so, certainly no one could dispute our claim to No. 1 after we won. The only team that has had that type of impressive march to a championship was Arizona in 1997 when it beat three No. 1 teams on its way to the title.

Against Indiana State, in the championship game, we were doing everything we wanted. Heathcote was a masterful coach and he decided to put 6-9 Earvin Johnson on the scouting team for our practice the day before the championship, so he could mimic the tendencies and skills of Larry Bird. Jud told Earvin to pass and shoot as much as he wanted. Johnson had an all-world shooting day in practice; he was shooting from all over the place. Jud was getting all over us because we wouldn't get out deep enough and check Earvin; but, again, that wasn't Larry Bird out there, it was Earvin Johnson, who had never hit shots like that before in his life. He hit them that day. Doing that gave us enough of a preview of what we needed to do the next night against the real Larry Bird.

Our strategy was to make sure there was a man on Bird at all times even though we were playing a match-up zone. We had a lot of communication in that zone in terms of always recognizing Bird's movements. When he would move to someone else's area of the zone, we would call out, "Okay Jay, he's yours." Then Jay would yell, "Okay Earvin, he's in your area; you've got him," and so forth. We were passing Bird around like a baton. Then when he would get the ball, we would send a second man at him. That was the respect we had for Larry Bird. We weren't about to let him beat us. We guarded him with one man when he didn't have the ball, and when he got the ball we guarded him with two men, then took our chances zoning up on everybody else.

It was a very frustrating night, for Bird, with that strategy. He shot 7-for-21, always with a hand in his face, and his passing lanes were cut to a minimum. He had decimated DePaul in the semifinals, hitting 16-of-19 shots on his way to 36 points. If we had let him get off like that against us, we couldn't have beaten Indiana State. Our defensive strategy worked, and offensively we were running, rebounding, and basically doing everything we wanted to do. We were taking high percentage shots, shooting 60 percent from the field for the game. Aside from the foul trouble that we encountered with both Earvin and me, we were able to accomplish everything that we wanted.

Final Four Fast Facts

In 1973, freshmen became eligible to compete at the varsity level.

That Indiana State game, with all due respect to those guys – they were undefeated and in their minds they felt like we just caught them on one of their off nights – would not have been as close as it was had I not picked up my fourth foul with about 16 minutes left in the game. I was out for nine minutes ... a very tough nine minutes sitting there watching that game. That was entirely too long of a breather. My fourth foul came on a very controversial call. Bird wasn't the quickest player defensively, but he kind of anticipated my move. I felt like he anticipated too late and he leaned in as I was going in for the shot, and there was contact. He sold it very well by going down, and the official called me for a charge. We lost 10 points of our 16-point lead in the next nine minutes.

We became a different team after the foul was called because we were trying to hold the ball and use up some of the clock. I truly believe that it could have been a 25-point (or more) game had Earvin and I not gotten into foul trouble. He managed to stay out of further foul trouble in the second half, but he did pick up three in the first half.

Looking back, this game had historical significance with the start of the "Magic" and Bird rivalry. From the Michigan State standpoint, we knew Earvin was special. It was apparent that he was going to be a tremendous player at the NBA level whenever he decided to go. He had always been a fantastic player at whatever level he was playing. I saw him as a high school player going against college guys and he was tremendous. When he became a college player, he was absolutely stunning in his grasp of the game, his knowledge of the game and certainly his control of the game. Then, throw in all of the charisma and everything mental that he brought to the court, and you've got just an unbelievable package.

So, we knew what Earvin was all about. I'm sure the guys on the Indiana State bench would say they felt the same about Larry Bird, having watched him every day in practice and witnessing his exploits in their games. We respected Bird as an opponent. He easily was one of the toughest guys we had to guard all year because, besides his shooting ability, he was 6-9, strong and deceptively quick. Looking at him, he doesn't look quick but his anticipation would give him that extra step. His quickness was in his mind; he was always thinking ahead. He was a tremendous shooter from all over the court. Bird could put the ball on the floor, he could rebound and he elevated the play of his teammates.

The Sycamores weren't a team full of hall of famers, yet, no one had beaten them all year. A lot of that can be attributed to Larry and his superb ability. He could absolutely do everything on the court, as we all know. There were other guys who may have had more impressive stats, but we never guarded anybody as tightly as we guarded Larry in the title game. That alone says he was a special player. I would have to say by and large, we knew that we were all fortunate to be a part of watching Earvin "Magic" Johnson and Larry Bird.

I was very fortunate to play with guys like Earvin and Jay Vincent; and be able to go to a Final Four and come away with a championship, especially in my senior year. You have to understand, though, that I expected to have that happen. I was aware that Michigan State hadn't been to the Final Four since 1957, the year I was born, with Johnny Green and those guys. While I was being recruited by Michigan State, one of the pitches that they used was that if I went there, and they signed a couple other key players, they would win a national championship before I graduated. Maybe I was naive, but it sounded good and I believed it. I became a Spartan in 1975.

As it turned out, not only did we sign one of those other key players in Earvin, but we also got Vincent who was a fantastic ball player. With those guys along with our other players, we were able to get to that Final Four.

Even now, I don't take that experience for granted. Sometimes when I look back I say to myself, "Wow, we should have actually gotten two championships." In my mind we were better than Kentucky the year before and lost to them in a game which we dominated. I quickly leave that thought alone, and think just how fortunate I am to have gotten the one title. When I look at all the great players over the years in college basketball who never got a chance to win a national championship, I really have to feel blessed. And I do, I truly do. Coaches are not limited to how many opportunities they can have to reach a Final Four, whereas players only get a maximum of four tries. I was lucky enough to cash in on my last.

Part IV: The '80S

CHAPTER 11

Indianapolis, Indiana
March 22 & 24, 1980

Oftentimes it is difficult to point to one player as making the difference in a game. However, in the 1980 semifinals between the Louisville Cardinals and Iowa Hawkeyes, it appeared as though one player might be the key to the game. Iowa's Ronnie Lester, who had missed nearly half of the season with a knee injury, scored his team's first 10 points of the game against Louisville. Midway through the first half, however, Lester went down with a season-ending knee injury.

Even though the momentum of the game didn't necessarily shift – it was a close score throughout – without Lester, the Hawkeyes didn't have that player they needed to counter Louisville's Darrell Griffith, who scored 34 points (and 23 points in the championship game).

The 1980 NCAA Tournament was Louisville head coach Denny Crum's seventh trip to the tournament (third to the Final Four) in nine seasons with the Cardinals. It was his third trip to the Final Four, but he had never reached the championship game. With a win over Iowa, the Cardinals met UCLA for the title.

Crum had prepared for the moment of reaching the championship game as a player at UCLA, and assistant coach at his alma mater to the legendary John Wooden. Ironically, in each of those three trips to the Final Four, Crum's teams met the Bruins. Three was the magic number as the Cardinals defeated the Bruins for the championship, 59-54. Through 1998-1999, the Cardinals have returned to the Final Four on three occasions ... they haven't faced the Bruins in the championship round since that 1980 title.

1980 All-Tournament Team

Joe Barry Carroll, Purdue
Rod Foster, UCLA
Darrell Griffith, Louisville
   (Most Outstanding Player)
Rodney McCray, Louisville
Kiki Vandeweghe, UCLA

Final Four Participants

Iowa
Louisville
Purdue
UCLA

National Semifinals

Louisville 80, Iowa 72
UCLA 67, Purdue 62

National Championship

Louisville 59, UCLA 54

Denny Crum

Iowa's Ronnie Lester, when he was healthy, was an outstanding player. As an opposing coach, I think what you have to do with a guy of his ability is have your team defense involved in handling him. He was good and he was difficult to guard one-on-one.

In our 1980 national semifinal game against the Hawkeyes, Lester, who had missed close to half of the 1979-1980 regular season with a knee injury, gave Louisville a scare by starting the game on fire. Our team had to be concerned when Ronnie scored his team's first 10 points of the game. In fact, at that point we had scored only 12 points as a team. We don't really want any opposing player to get off to a good start, because if we can jump on a team early, contain it and not ever let it get unwound, that's a big bonus. Even if our team is not playing real well or scoring, as long as our opponent is doing the same thing, we are at least in the game. With Lester's help, Iowa was very much in the game, trailing 12-10.

At that level of college basketball, defense is usually what wins games. So, when somebody gets off to a good start, there is definite reason for concern. Coaches can have a major problem when somebody starts a game hot against them, and it seems that no matter what that player does, it turns out right. With one individual player, if that's the go-to guy and he can be contained, then we are obviously going to be a lot better off. When Ronnie got hurt during the season, the Hawkeyes had to rely on other people. That is what they did during the course of the season and did quite well. Obviously they were better with Lester than without him. Unfortunately for the Hawkeyes, they had to go back to find a new go-to guy in the semifinals ... Lester went down with a season-ending knee injury. As had been the case throughout the regular season without Lester, that go-to guy became Kenny Arnold. In our semifinal game, Arnold led the Hawkeye scorers with 20 points.

When Ronnie left the game with about eight minutes left in the first half, there didn't seem to be a big shift in momentum toward either team. A lot of times when a key player gets hurt or fouls out, everybody else on that team gives that much more effort. They know that somebody has to step up because they have lost an integral part of their team.

Many times a player's injury can cause a team to go the other way, and they lose all confidence in themselves and things kind of go haywire. I don't know how to predict what's going to happen. In Iowa's case it didn't seem to affect them either way. They weren't as good of a team physically without Lester, but how much that had to do with the final outcome of the game, would certainly be speculation. They were definitely a better team with him. The Hawkeyes have to be admired for the fact that they got where they were, for the most part, without Ronnie.

After Ronnie's injury from earlier in the season, I don't think he got back to the point where he was 100 percent, but he had the ability and the opportunity to play in the Final Four. Considering he had been hurt and was rehabilitating, Ronnie may have put a lot of burden on himself throughout the tournament.

The one nice thing about the way the tournament is set up today (and in 1980), seeding is not based on where a team was during the season; it's where they are at the end of the year. Among the 1980 Final Four teams of Purdue, Iowa, UCLA and Louisville, we were the only conference champions that got there. The other teams received at-large berths. That's interesting because in Iowa's case, when they got Ronnie back, he played very well for them and moved them up another level.

His play enabled them to be at their best at year-end, and they finished really strong. Without Ronnie they may not have reached the tournament. He was an outstanding player.

People probably underestimate the value of any one player in the team concept of basketball. Think about it. If a football team loses one player, excluding a good quarterback who is more valuable, they lose 1/22 of their team – 11 offense and 11 defense. In basketball, if a team loses one player, at least 20 percent is gone, while a really good player on a given night can be the equivalent of 30-50 percent of a team in terms of his output. It's really hard to overcome the loss of any one individual basketball player.

We had the same scenario at Louisville in 1977. We played Marquette, who later that season won the national championship, on its home floor and beat them. We won 15 games in a row; I thought we were the best team in the country. Then, Larry Williams, our starting forward, broke his foot with six games to go in the season, and we were never the same. We lost in the first round of the NCAA Tournament.

It's a real credit to Iowa, how much Ronnie helped them even though he wasn't 100 percent. When you think in terms of guarding and playing a team with a guy of Lester's caliber, you know that it is going to be better because of him, so everybody on defense has got to be conscious of him. That meant that his teammates stepped up their game. He was so quick, he really was an outstanding player.

I don't remember any major shift of any kind in the game when Lester went down. Both teams were playing really hard and trying to get a good lead; everybody wanted to win to get to that championship game. His teammates didn't let him down in the first half. The Hawkeyes were down by only five, 34-29, at the break.

Our Louisville squad was such a young team heading into that season, that one of the few bright spots was that we had a great player in senior Darrell Griffith. In a lot of ways, he was our team's equivalent to Ronnie Lester. We were made up of a freshman center at 6-foot-6, Rodney McCray, three sophomores and Griffith. I thought we had enough good athletes in practice every day that by the end of the year, we would be pretty good. At the beginning of the season, the Final Four seemed like a long way for our group. One good thing was that we had some pretty good basketball players on the second team, practicing with the other guys and improving in our system that way. Since a team practices 130-some days in the year for three hours at a time, but it only plays 30 games consisting of 40 minutes, the time and effort spent in practice is very important to development. If a team is competitive and has really competitive, hard-nosed practices, its chances of getting to a

Final Four are a lot better.

The beauty of our team throughout the whole 1980 tournament was the fact that every time we got in a pinch, the guys never lost confidence because they knew Darrell would step up and do something.

There was one exception as I recall when Darrell didn't come through, but the team found it could count on another player. We played Kansas State in our first game of the tournament, and Darrell fouled out in the second half. I put in Tony Branch, who had been a starter for us, and then in his senior year was beaten out by Jerry Eaves, a sophomore. Tony had a super attitude about being beaten out of his spot because he was such a team-oriented player. He felt that as long as he kept working hard, good things would happen. Boy, was he right. When Darrell fouled out of the Kansas State game, Tony stepped up and hit the winning shot for us in overtime. Had he not hit that shot, giving us the 71-69 win, we may not have made it out of the first round. That was the only game where we really needed Griffith and he wasn't there. Although, in the regional finals we faced Louisiana State, when they were ranked second in the country, and Darrell only played 14 minutes because of foul trouble. We beat the Tigers by 20.

The kids had a lot of confidence in themselves, but they had a tremendous amount of confidence in Darrell. They knew that if things got tough, he would step up and do something – usually spectacular – because he was such a great athlete. He could run and jump, and as his shooting improved, he was really hard to guard. Because of that, we went to him in a lot of situations, including the championship game at a couple of crucial spots. We simply called his play and got the ball to him.

In Darrell's day, there weren't many who could jump like him, although now there seems to be quite a few of them. In his day he was kind of a phenom who could really get up in the air. I'll never forget when I was asked after the 1980 Olympic tryouts, how high Darrell could jump. I told them he jumped as high as he wanted to. That seemed to be the truth. They measured his vertical jump at around 44 inches. He could take off with his heel hitting just inside the free throw line, and dunk the ball even though he couldn't palm it like Michael Jordan, who has great big hands. That's not too bad for a player who was only 6-foot-2 1/2. (He was listed at 6-foot-4, but I know he's not that tall.) He's not real big, but he played big. Because Darrell had small hands and couldn't palm a basketball, he had to cup it between his hand and wrist. He was still phenomenal with the things he could do because of his jumping ability. I would much rather have a 6-2 kid who can jump 40 inches than have a 6-5 kid who can jump 25 inches.

Darrell always seemed to be doing something sensational on the court. In the championship game, against UCLA, we were down five points late in the second half. We called a special play for him, where we ran him underneath the basket, hit the post man with a pass, and Darrell pins the defender behind and we throw it in. Well, he was being guarded by Michael Holton, who jumped in front of Darrell, causing us not to be able to get the play going. Instinctively, Darrell turned his back, put his hand up and Wiley Brown threw him the ball up by the rim. Griffith jumped up, caught the ball and put it in while he was up there. He was fouled in the process and hit the free throw. That was a three-point play at a crucial time, bringing us back to within two. There is a whole lot of difference between being down two and being down five. Just one basket ties it up. (This was before the introduction of the three-point line.) We went on to score the last nine points of the game, including five from Darrell, and won 59-54.

During our 80-72 win over Iowa in the semifinals, Darrell played the majority of the game and scored 34 points. In the finals, the game in which he went on that run at the end of the second half, he played 38 minutes and scored 23 points. Rightly so, Griffith ended up being the Most Valuable Player of the tournament. It was a fitting end to his remarkable career.

Darrell was a very special player with a great attitude. He graduated in four years and did everything that he could to succeed on and off the court. I never once had to discipline him in any shape or form. He was just a great individual and a heck of a player.

One of the sophomores on that Louisville team was left-handed Wiley Brown. When Brown was 3 years old, there was an accident and most of his right thumb had to be removed. Since the accident happened at such a young age, he grew up doing things with his left hand. (Whether he would have been left-handed anyway, who knows.) When he came to Louisville, we had a prosthesis, or artificial thumb, made for him to wear when he was playing. Then, to help him during games, we cut out all of the fingers, except for the thumb, on stretchy, surgical gloves. Three or four of those were put on his hand to hold the prosthesis in place. He usually got taped and had his hand prepared right after the pregame meal.

Before the Iowa game, Wiley accidentally left the prosthesis on the dining table after we ate. When they got ready to tape him, he realized he wasn't wearing the thumb. He called the trainer. When they went back to where we ate, the table had already been cleaned off, and the thumb had been thrown out because they thought it was part of the garbage. To make matters worse, the garbage can was already emptied out back into the big garbage container. There we were – the whole team – going through the garbage trying to find Wiley's prosthetic thumb. Luckily, they finally found it. The story is funny now, but at the time it wasn't because Brown played so much better with the artificial thumb. He could rebound and catch the ball a whole lot better.

Wiley is also credited, along with teammates Derek Smith and Daryl Cleveland, with introducing the world to the high-five. They did it on television for the first time after we won the 1980 title. They're all from Georgia; Derek was from Hogansville, Daryl was from Thomasville and Wiley was from Sylvester. In fact, after we won the championship we were invited to the White House. Jimmy Carter, from Georgia, was the president. When we went into the oval office, the team presented President Carter with a signed basketball and those three gave him a T-shirt from the "Georgia Connection." The president said he wanted to congratulate the Louisville team and especially the "Georgia Connection." That was a lot of fun.

Our 1980 squad proved that it was definitely ready for the tournament. Personally, having spent time at UCLA as John Wooden's assistant, and going to the Final Four with them, helped me prepare to take Louisville to those finals. Coach Wooden's philosophy was that we did the same things in practice the day before the final game of the NCAA championship that we did in the first week of practice, and the middle of the season. He believed in teaching the fundamentals of the game all season. He was a great teacher who believed in doing the things that you need to do and don't worry too much about your opponent. That way you just keep getting better and better at the things you do. That's how he prepared. When I have had my Louisville teams in the Final Four, I've approached our preparation in that same way.

A lot of times teams get so concerned about an opponent, and kids get so focused on one opponent, that they forget and don't do the things they're supposed to do. Coaches have to be really careful about that when it comes down to the Final Four. We have to be careful about it for any game, but tournament games are so big and crucial to everyone that it's real easy to lose focus on what we're doing because we are so concerned about one opponent.

We have been in Final Fours that we didn't win. That's not uncommon for any coach or team, including Coach Wooden. A lot of times just getting to that stage is a real bonus, but it gets to the point where everybody who doesn't win the thing now is unhappy. In many instances, if you would have told them before the season started that they were going to be a Final Four team, they would have been tickled to death. But at the end of the year, having gotten that far and not won, which is the case for three teams, they feel let down. Getting there is certainly a great achievement and you've got to feel good about that, even if it is hard to be happy when the season ends with a loss.

Reaching a Final Four is very difficult to do without good competition in practice and not playing a tough schedule, because come tournament time, winning six consecutive games is really tough. That can't be simulated in a regular season unless the schedule is tough. We have always tried to schedule tough games – as tough as we can – so that by year's end we will have played a lot of the top teams, regardless of who they are, which should help us be a better team. Even if we lose those games, we at least find out what our team can and cannot do. In 1980, we lost only three games. In our championship season of 1986, we had seven losses, but we won our last 10 games of the season, which included the six needed in the NCAA Tournament. My personal opinion is that playing tough regular season games will help at tournament time.

Playing a tough schedule helped our team mature throughout 1979-1980 and helped us through a couple of tough NCAA Tournament games. I've always said that to get to a Final Four, unless you are just totally dominating, and you are much better physically than every one else, you have to either be a little lucky or have no bad luck. Games can turn out that way. The whole complexion of the game, and the final outcome, can be changed with a bad call, one instant or one play that goes the wrong way.

I learned an awful lot of things from Coach Wooden. Having been involved in three championships at UCLA and then watching the others, I felt qualified to lead our team to the title in 1980. Our kids came through when they needed to play well. Their hard work and dedication paid off with a national championship.

CHAPTER 12

New Orleans, Louisiana
March 27 & 29, 1982

CBS Sports picked up the television rights for the NCAA tournament in 1982. The network could not have hand-picked a better championship game to welcome college basketball fans. Even though the championship game with North Carolina and Georgetown, two No. 1 seeds, introduced the world to a freshman named Michael Jordan, with his now-famous jumpshot from the wing with 17 seconds remaining to help beat Georgetown, the game had several other key elements. In fact, more people probably remember what happened after Jordan's shot, than remember "the shot," when Georgetown's Fred Brown made an ill-advised pass straight to Carolina's James Worthy in the final seconds of the game to seal the Hoyas' fate.

Besides having several future NBA players on the court that night in the Superdome, the game featured two future Hall of Famers, Jordan and Georgetown's Patrick Ewing. It is a game that fans wish they still had on videotape. This also was the first year that the losing teams from the semifinal game did not play each other in the national third place game.

Woody Durham is nearing his 30th year as the "Voice of the Tar Heels." He was with legendary coach Dean Smith for all but 274 of Smith's 879 career victories. Durham says he still has his score sheets from March 29, 1982, framed and hanging in his office.

Final Four Fast Facts

The 1976 semifinal game featured three of that year's five All-Americans: Kent Benson and Scott May from Indiana, and UCLA's Richard Washington.

1982 All-Tournament Team

Patrick Ewing, Georgetown
Eric Floyd, Georgetown
Michael Jordan, North Carolina
Sam Perkins, North Carolina
James Worthy, North Carolina
   (Most Outstanding Player)

Final Four Participants

Georgetown
Houston
Louisville
North Carolina

National Semifinals

North Carolina 68, Houston 63
Georgetown 50, Louisville 46

National Championship

UNC 63, Georgetown 62

Woody Durham

When Michael Jordan first came to Carolina in the fall of 1981, he had a jacket from his high school days which had the name "Magic" on the back of it. He was in the basketball office one day wearing that jacket. Coach Dean Smith came out of his office, walked by Jordan, gave something to the secretary, spoke to Michael a minute, then walked back toward his office. (Coach had a way of saying just the right thing to make a point.)

He turned to Michael and said, "You know if I were you, I think I'd get my own nickname." Then he walked back into his office. I don't believe Michael ever wore that jacket again.

Carolina was ranked No.1 in the 1981-1982 preseason by a couple of polls, including *Sports Illustrated*. Going into the season, the Tar Heels had lost only one player, Al Wood, from the previous year's team which made it to the NCAA championship game against Indiana. It stands to reason they would be viewed as the top team in the country. The *Sports Illustrated* college basketball issue featured the four returning starters (James Worthy, Sam Perkins, Matt Doherty and Jimmy Black) on the cover. Coach Smith had a policy that before a freshman played his first regular-season game, he was not to talk with the media. Since Michael had not played a game when the cover picture was taken, Coach did not feel he should be included. (That's one *Sports Illustrated* cover that Michael Jordan didn't make.)

Buzz Peterson, the current head coach at Appalachian State University, had been the North Carolina High School Player of the Year from Asheville, and was in the freshman recruiting class with Michael, who was from Wilmington, N.C. Shortly after the team had started its preseason practices, I asked Coach how things were going. He said, "I think this young guy from Wilmington is going to be able to help us quite a bit." That's probably one of the biggest understatements in the history of the game.

Jordan was a pretty good player as a freshman. There certainly weren't signs of him becoming the "greatest to ever play the game," but throughout that season he was a perfect addition to the team, in what he brought to the squad as the big guard. He was the fifth starter on the 1982 team, making him only the fourth freshman under Coach Smith to start his first game for Carolina. During Coach Smith's 36-year career at Carolina, only nine players started their first game as a freshman, including Phil Ford, Mike O'Koren, Worthy, Jordan, Kenny Smith, J.R. Reid, Vince Carter, Antawn Jamison and Ed Cota. Those players started because they had earned that right in practice. Pete Chilcutt, Rick Fox and Brendan Haywood started their first games only because two regular starters missed the bus and another was late getting to the pregame meal.

The Tar Heels lost two regular season games in 1981-82. The first defeat was at home against Wake Forest, 55-48. Although the Demon Deacons played awfully well, Perkins and his 14.3 points per game average missed the game because of a virus. Then, about two weeks later, Carolina lost to Ralph Sampson and Virginia in Charlottesville, 74-58.

Carolina did receive redemption against Virginia in the finals of the ACC Tournament. The Tar Heels beat the Cavaliers, 47-45, and people point to that game for bringing about the shot clock. The Tar Heels spread out their offense in an attempt to draw Sampson out from under the basket. Virginia chose to leave Sampson underneath and did not come out to pressure Carolina. Coach Smith simply wanted his team to take the most high percentage shots it could get.

Late in the game, the Cavaliers wanted to put the Tar Heels at the free-throw line. I recall, since they hadn't committed enough fouls to put the Tar Heels in the bonus, it took the Cavaliers nearly two minutes to commit the needed fouls. They started fouling with 3:30 remaining and had to keep fouling until about the 1:30 mark before the Tar Heels went to the free-throw line.

That win gave Carolina the No. 1 seed in the East Region, with early round games in Charlotte and the regional championship in Raleigh. After a narrow victory over James Madison in Charlotte, and victories in Raleigh against Alabama and Villanova, the Tar Heels downed Houston in the national semifinals and made it into the championship game against Georgetown. The Hoyas, the top seed in the West, had lost six games during the regular season, but had cruised through the tournament behind seven-foot-freshman center Patrick Ewing and senior guard Sleepy Floyd.

There has been so much focus through the years on the last 31 seconds of the 1982 title game with Jordan's shot and Fred Brown's errant pass to Worthy, it has taken away from what was a terrific basketball game. Georgetown never led by more than four points and Carolina was never ahead by more than three points.

Looking at the 10 players in the starting lineups, five went on to have a big impact on the game of basketball. From Georgetown, Ewing is still very much a force in the National Basketball Association (NBA), while Floyd had an outstanding NBA career. From Carolina, Jordan is considered to be the best ever to play the game, while both Worthy and Sam Perkins had stellar careers in the NBA.

Going into the championship game, Coach Smith had instructed the Tar Heels to take the ball directly at Ewing. Carolina wanted to quickly bring the ball up the floor, and get it to the baseline to attack Georgetown's pressure defense. The Tar Heels knew Ewing would be a force inside, but their plan was solid. As a result, he was called for five goaltending violations in the early stages of the game, with Worthy taking most of those shots. Carolina's first eight points of the game were goaltending calls against Ewing. However, Georgetown held a brief advantage, 32-31, at the half.

The second half became physical. Sleepy Floyd and Jimmy Black were involved in a little altercation with some pushing and shoving. Worthy had grown up in Gastonia, N.C., as did Floyd, but they went to different high schools. Yet they had known each other for a long time. One play after the Floyd-Black incident, Buzz Peterson came up with a steal and passed ahead to Worthy. Floyd was back defending for the Hoyas – a big mistake. Worthy slam-dunked the ball so hard, it came out of the net and hit Floyd right on top of the head. Worthy didn't say a word when that happened, but it seemed he had sent a message to Floyd. Don't mess with Jimmy Black or any of his other Carolina teammates.

Late in the game, Jordan hit one of the most difficult shots in his young collegiate career. No, not the shot that everyone remembers, but one which was more difficult. As he drove in the lane Ewing was there defensively, but Michael went up in the air, and released the ball over the top of Ewing's outstretched hand and banked it off the top of the square. When Jordan hit that shot, Coach Smith grabbed assistant coach Bill Guthridge's arm and said, "Did you see that?!" That was a more impossible shot, in my opinion, than the one he made to actually win the game.

1982 Final, North Carolina vs. Georgetown

With 57 seconds left, Floyd hit a shot to put Georgetown up, 62-61. Dean Smith always had a reputation for not taking a late timeout, when his team had a chance to pull out a win. However, he called this timeout – with 31 seconds remaining – because he felt his team was hesitant against the Hoyas' passive press.

In late game situations, Dean Smith always wanted to take shots with enough time on the clock that if the shot missed, the Tar Heels would have a chance to rebound and put it back in for a possible win. Smith didn't feel Georgetown coach John Thompson, his long-time friend, was going to let Perkins and Worthy get open down low. Jordan would probably be the one to shoot, and either Perkins or Worthy should be in good position for the rebound. When the team broke the timeout huddle, Coach Smith told the guys to hit the boards, but he knew deep down Michael Jordan was going to have to take the shot from the wing after the ball rotated around the perimeter the second time. When Michael left the huddle, Coach slapped him on the rump and told him to make the shot.

As the play transpired, it happened just as Coach Smith had expected. The patient Tar Heels rotated the ball around the perimeter trying to find an open shot for Worthy or Perkins. Then Black threw the ball to Jordan on the left wing. He fired up a jump shot from the wing with 17 seconds remaining and hit it. If Jordan missed short, Perkins was all alone under the board. During an interview I did with Coach Smith after the season, he said they had actually wanted to take a shot with more than 17 seconds left, going back to the idea of having enough time to possibly get a rebound and try again to score.

Years later I was introducing Michael's mother at a charity function and said, "Neither one of us would probably have been here tonight, and this wouldn't have been going on, if it hadn't been for that shot in 1982 in New Orleans." She later acknowledged that idea by saying, "I've often thought we probably wouldn't have had the opportunity for all of this to happen if it hadn't been for that shot. It not only brought Carolina the national championship, but it brought Michael recognition, too."

With 15 seconds remaining and down by one point, 63-62, Georgetown still had plenty of time. They had one timeout, which Thompson elected not to use, in order for his team to get the ball up court as quickly as possible.

In order to completely explain the next play, I need to fast forward a little. About three weeks after the national championship, I stopped by the basketball office one afternoon, and assistant coach Eddie Fogler was watching the film of the game. When I stuck my head in the door, he said, "Come here, I want to show you something." He showed me the

Georgetown possession after Jordan scored.

The clock was winding down on the Hoyas, and guard Fred Brown knew he had to get rid of the ball. He wanted to make a pass to the right baseline to either Floyd or Eric Smith. As he prepared to make that pass, Jordan, who was at the top of the defense along with Black, took one step to his left and blocked Brown's passing lane to the baseline. Fogler said that Jordan probably did it instinctively, but whatever the reason, that's when Brown panicked.

As the clock ran down, Brown needed to find someone who could shoot the ball (because he knew that he wasn't the guy to do it), the passing lane had been cut-off by Jordan, and Ewing was heavily guarded inside. As a result, Brown threw it to the first open white jersey he saw. Luckily for Carolina, the white uniform happened to be that of James Worthy. Just before that pass, for some unknown reason, Worthy started to break away from his defensive position. (To this day I have no idea why he did it, because his move certainly wasn't part of the defense.) James told me later that he never called Fred Brown by name to warrant the pass. Basically, Brown just did it. The only explanation I have for it is that he caught a glimpse of a white uniform moving to the outside, and threw it to the uniform. Up until that game, as the higher seeded team in its region, Georgetown had worn white uniforms, but in the Carolina game the Hoyas were wearing their blue uniforms.

As a broadcaster, and a graduate of the University of North Carolina, it was difficult maintaining my composure while this was happening. Before Brown's "pass" to Worthy, I had been quickly recalling previous seasons. The Tar Heels had suffered real disappointment in 1977, in Atlanta, losing that final 67-59 to Marquette. It was a year Carolina had won 15 straight games and had endured key injuries. That was the last game Marquette's Al McGuire coached, so the Tar Heels had to contend with that emotion on the opposing side. Yet, it was still a game in which the thought of losing the title didn't occur until Carolina actually lost that night.

Then, the Tar Heels reached the championship game in 1981, in Philadelphia, after beating Ralph Sampson and Virginia in the semifinals but they lost to the Indiana Hoosiers and their great point guard, Isiah Thomas, in the finals.

Those were big disappointments. Since the Hoyas still had time to score after Jordan's shot, it wasn't quite time to celebrate. I was sitting there trying to get my thoughts together as to what I was going to say if Carolina held on to win, but also what I would say if Georgetown got the ball inside to Ewing or someone else hit an outside shot for the win. About that time, not more than 20 feet in front of me, Brown threw the ball right to Worthy. I must admit at that stage, I really started to lose it emotionally to say, "How about them Heels ... they're going to win the national championship!" That's the only thing I have in my memory bank that I had planned to say when the outcome was definite. Worthy was fouled with a couple of seconds left, and of course the Carolina fans in the Louisiana Superdome were going crazy.

Down at the Carolina bench, Coach Smith was calling the players toward him. He realized the game was not over. James still had to shoot his free throws. Coach wanted to calm everyone down and tell them what to do defensively if James missed the two shots. As it turns out, James *did* miss *both* of the free throws. After getting the rebound, Floyd threw up a desperation shot from the backcourt for the Hoyas that missed. Perkins caught the ball and threw it in the air. By then it was over and the Tar Heels had won! Those last few seconds were very emotional and very tense because even though it looked like Carolina had the game won, Coach Smith was not ready to celebrate. He was probably the calmest person in the building. Everybody else who followed Carolina, myself included, were losing it.

That was the first of Dean Smith's two national championships. It's interesting that both games had an unusual play by the opposition to help determine the outcome, as well as an unacknowledged defensive play by a Tar Heel. In 1982, it was Brown's pass to Worthy following Jordan's move into Brown's passing lane. In the 1993 game, also in New Orleans, Michigan's Chris Webber rebounded a missed free throw with about 20 seconds left in the game and the Tar Heels leading, 73-71. He was going to make an outlet pass to Jalen Rose, but Carolina's George Lynch got in the passing lane. At that same time, for some unknown reason, the entire Michigan team ran away from Webber. When Lynch jumped in the passing lane, Webber dragged his foot (but wasn't called for traveling!), and he delayed long enough so that Lynch and Derrick Phelps were able to trap him in a tight double-team in the corner. Webber's teammates had all run toward the other side of the court, so he had nobody to whom he could pass the ball, and he called a timeout. Michigan didn't have any timeouts remaining, so the Wolverines were charged with a technical. Webber later said that someone from the Michigan bench yelled, "Timeout! Timeout!" So, he called one. There's probably been more made of the timeout called by Webber than maybe there should have been. Carolina still had fouls to give, so I don't think the Wolverines would have gotten a shot off even if Webber didn't make his mistake. It is interesting, though, the similarity between both '82 and '93.

After the Michigan game, Coach Smith got to the locker room before the players and wrote on the chalkboard, "No practice tomorrow.

Congratulations!" His message was a perfect end to a perfect season.

I find it odd that not a lot of attention has been given to Michael Jordan stepping into the passing lane of Fred Brown in 1982, or to George Lynch stepping into the passing lane of Chris Webber in 1993. Those were big defensive plays.

Both titles were won in the Louisiana Superdome in New Orleans. Oddly, the Tar Heels were one game away from going back to New Orleans in 1987, but they lost to Syracuse in the regional finals. Indiana beat Syracuse for the national title on a last-second shot by Keith Smart. Who knows what would have happened if Carolina had been there?

Oh, and that nickname of "Magic" ... By the time he completed his freshman season in 1982, Michael Jordan certainly was on his way toward his own nickname.

CHAPTER 13

Albuquerque, New Mexico
April 2 & 4, 1983

The 1983 version of the Houston Cougars had been a great team most of the season, losing only twice. They were led by super players such as Hakeem Olajuwon, Michael Young, Larry Micheaux and Clyde Drexler. They seemed to be improved from their 1982 team that lost in the national semifinals to eventual champion, North Carolina.

The only problem for the Cougars was that they were set to face a team of destiny in North Carolina State in the championship game. The Wolfpack were coached by a relatively unknown, fiery guy by the name of Jim Valvano.

Cougar head coach Guy Lewis had reached the Final Four on three previous occasions, but had not been to the championship game. Lewis, who played for the Cougars in 1946 and 1947 before serving as head coach from 1956-1986, now enjoys the retired life in Texas. He was honored when the University of Houston named the Hofheinz Pavilion basketball floor the "Guy V. Lewis Court" in 1995.

1983 All-Tournament Team

Thurl Bailey, NCSU
Sidney Lowe, NCSU
Akeem Olajuwon, Houston
   (Most Outstanding Player)
Milt Wagner, Louisville
Dereck Whittenberg, NCSU

Final Four Participants

Georgia
Houston
Louisville
North Carolina State

National Semifinals

Houston 94, Louisville 81
NCSU 67, Georgia 60

National Championship

NCSU 54, Houston 52

113

Stories From the Final Four: The '80s

Guy Lewis

To understand our thoughts on the North Carolina State championship game in 1983, I need to mention the semifinal game with Louisville on that Saturday. The Louisville game didn't appear to be close on the scoreboard, 94-81, but it was such a high-powered game with a lot of running and defensive pressure, that at the end we were totally fatigued. (Louisville was in worse shape than us because two of their guys had to go to the hospital from dehydration.)

We had a very light workout on Sunday because our guys were dead. That was such a contrast from the week before when we had a high-powered game against Memphis in the regionals. I cut practice short the day after that game because we had so much energy that it was flowing, and I wanted to save some of it for the regional finals. We came out and beat Villanova, 89-71, for a trip to the Final Four.

Things were completely different after the Louisville game the next week. Houston and Louisville were very similar teams in the way we played; we both ran a lot and pressed a lot. We were losing to the Cardinals, 41-36, at halftime, but came back in the second half and won the game going away, 94-81, in what many consider to be one of the greatest Final Four games ever played. We were dead tired after that game.

At our pregame meal on Monday, I was mainly talking about us instead of North Carolina State. I was more worried about how we were going to do physically than I was about what the Wolfpack were going to do against us. I tried to explain to the team how North Carolina State, which seemed to be a team of destiny, had to win the Atlantic Coast Conference tournament to get into the NCAA tournament; and how they had beaten Pepperdine in the opening round in double-overtime after being down by six with a couple of minutes to play in regulation. That was a big game because we had played Pepperdine earlier in the year and had won by only one point. I also knew how good Jerry Tarkanian's UNLV team was that North Carolina State came from behind to beat.

Everybody talked about how we were favored against N.C. State, but I never felt like we were the favorite. I was really worried about the game. My players would say that I was worried about every game we ever played, but I was especially concerned with the Wolfpack.

I expected N.C. State to play a slow-down game. They played a controlled game, but they certainly weren't passing up shots to hold the ball. Just like in the semifinal game, we were behind at the half. This time, the Wolfpack led, 33-25.

1983 Final, North Carolina State vs. Houston

We opened the second half with a 17-2 run to take a seven-point lead. Unfortunately I had to take Hakeem Olajuwon out of the game to give him oxygen because he was having so many problems breathing. As the second half progressed, and we had the lead, we tried to slow the tempo down on offense to give the guys a breather. I have been criticized frequently for running that slow-down offense, but we weren't in it for very long (although it may have looked like it since we were sluggish on the floor). We ran three different offenses in the game, each equally ineffective.

We had a seven-point lead toward the end of the game, but N.C. State started fouling us. That turned out to be a smart move because we couldn't hit our free throws (we finished the game 10-19 on free-throw attempts). That gave them a chance to catch up. I always felt like North Carolina State was in the ballgame. They wouldn't go away, even after that 17-2 run to start the second half. Thank goodness the 3-point shot wasn't in effect then because most of the shots they were making were from long range. They were making their shots and we were missing our free throws ... that was the whole difference in the game.

On the last possession, they called a timeout at which time I switched to a half-court trapping defense. Through the years, that scheme bailed us out of a ton of ballgames that could have been losses. We nearly had a steal against Dereck Whittenberg, but he got the ball back and threw up that shot (everybody wanted to claim that it was a pass, but it was definitely a shot). When Hakeem saw that we almost stole the ball, he broke to the other end of the court. Unfortunately, Whittenberg got the ball back and shot it, and there was Lorenzo Charles open under the basket, waiting to stuff it in.

During my coaching career, we took five teams to the Final Four. In each of the five trips, we lost to the team that eventually won the tournament. Unfortunately a coach can get more criticism for going 31-2 during the season and losing in the finals than he can for not having a winning season. I've experienced that.

Before we reached that first Final Four in 1967, I wondered if we were ever going to make it. When we finally made it, it was like a dream come true. To go back the very next year was another tremendous thrill. It was 14 years before we made it back. I don't mind saying that during that drought I had my doubts as to whether or not we would ever reach the Final Four again. Then we went three times in a row.

The first one, in 1967, was the most important, but my fifth one, in 1984, would be in a close second-place. I got so much criticism after losing in 1983, that going back in 1984 was a big deal.

I got a call one day in 1977 from the Director of the Basketball Hall of Fame, wanting all of the teams to pass around a bucket during their home games to collect money for the Hall of Fame. I told him that I had an idea of how to raise a lot more money than they were collecting with a hat being passed around at ballgames, and we wouldn't be humiliating ourselves. We met a couple weeks later at the Athletic Director's convention (I was assistant A.D. at Houston) in Las Vegas.

The NCAA had a rule that a team could not start playing its games before December 1, and it couldn't schedule more than 28 games in the season. My idea was to get the NCAA to give an exemption to the two teams that played in the Hall of Fame game from both of those rules. That way they could play the game the last weekend in November to open the season, and it wouldn't count against their schedule. I told the Hall of Fame Director that I thought most schools would play in that game for the cost of expenses. Needless to say, Houston was the first volunteer.

Our Athletic Director got the idea passed through the other A.D.s, and they took it to the NCAA where it also passed. The only thing about the new set up was that we weren't invited for several years. Ironically, we were invited to play in it the year after we lost to North Carolina State. The first team we played in the Hall of Fame game, in 1983-1984, was North Carolina State. They beat us again in that game, by 12 points. It wasn't close.

We looked so bad in that Hall of Fame game that I couldn't wait to get back home to work out my team. We did everything wrong in that game. We were so bad that it looked like we might not win a game all season. Instead, a week later we beat Kansas by

In 1999, Connecticut became the first school since 1966 (UTEP) to win the national championship on its first trip to the Final Four..

15 points. The Cougars went on to have a very good year, losing only three more times and advancing to the national championship game where we lost to Georgetown, 84-75.

After that terrible start, it felt almost as good to get back to the Final Four that fifth time, as getting there the first time.

Going to the Final Four is a great thrill. I've always felt that the Saturday of the Final Four, with all four teams playing, and their fans thinking that their team has a chance to win, is the most exciting sporting event, year-in and year-out, that we have in the country.

I haven't missed a Final Four since I've retired and I don't plan to miss any. In fact, 1999 was my 44th consecutive Final Four. Even though they keep moving the ex-coaches further and further away from the court (in the next couple years we'll be out of the gym), I still get a huge thrill out of going and being a part of the excitement.

A bonus to being at the game is that I don't have to see the end of the 1983 title game. They show that last play of the game on television every year during the Final Four. The first thing that comes to my mind when I see it is to turn off the TV. I've lived my life pretty well without that shot ... I don't need to look at it anymore.

CHAPTER 14

Lexington, Kentucky
March 30 & April 1, 1985

U nderdog. Cinderella. Snowball's chance. These are all terms that have been used to describe the Villanova Wildcats and their 1985 national championship win over the Georgetown Hoyas, the No. 1 team in the country.

The Wildcats entered the NCAA Tournament with 10 losses, and went in as a No. 8 seed. While people were still shaking their heads, trying to figure out how the Wildcats received an at-large berth, the team was starting to make some noise. After a last-second shot helped them escape their opening round opponent, Dayton, the Wildcats upset the top-seeded Michigan Wolverines.

When the team eventually reached the Final Four with wins over two No. 2 seeds, North Carolina and Memphis State, it was squared off with Big East Conference foe Georgetown.

Steve Lappas was a first-year assistant coach on that 1985 Villanova team. Even though everyone is excited about their Final Four experience, especially the winners, Lappas is certainly one of the most fired-up. After taking a hiatus as head coach at Manhattan, Lappas was named the Villanova head coach on April 14, 1992, where he continues to try to get the Wildcats back to the Final Four.

1985 All-Tournament Team

Patrick Ewing, Georgetown
Harold Jensen, Villanova
Dwayne McClain, Villanova
Gary McLain, Villanova
Ed Pinckney, Villanova
  (Most Outstanding Player)

Final Four Participants

Georgetown
Memphis State
St. John's
Villanova

National Semifinals

Georgetown 77, St. John's 59
Villanova 52, Memphis State 45

National Championship

Villanova 66, Georgetown 64

Steve Lappas

Each year I had a party at my house to watch the Final Four. As we were watching the 1984 tournament, I said, "What I wouldn't give to have a ticket to the Final Four." The next year I was on the bench as a first-year assistant with Villanova! For me, that was the most unbelievable thing. If someone would have told me that night at my house in Jackson Heights that the next year I was going to be sitting on the bench during the Final Four, I would have thought they were out of their mind. But, that's what happened.

I had interviewed for several other assistant's jobs at schools like Lehigh, Columbia and Manhattan, but got turned down. Each rejection left me distraught. Then, to get the job at Villanova and win the NCAA championship in my first year, is incredible!

It was an unbelievable experience to be there. I was just along for the ride, getting the coffee and the sneakers, making copies of scouting reports, those types of first-year assistant coach duties. I had nothing to do with the team's success.

The 1985 Villanova Wildcats were certainly a team of destiny. Not only did we shoot out of our minds at 79 percent from the field in the championship game against the Georgetown Hoyas, we won our first three games of the tournament by a total margin of nine points. On top of that, we shot around 40 percent during three of our five other tournament games, and still won. That is unheard of. We had great defensive schemes, though, which was the key to keeping us in ballgames.

There was a lot of destiny involved in that team.

We didn't consider ourselves underdogs or favorites or anything else, going into the 1985 NCAA Tournament. We simply knew that we could play with anybody in the country because the players had competed well against some of the top teams. Ed Pinckney, Dwayne McClain and Gary McLain were on the Villanova team that went to the Elite Eight in 1983. Because of that NCAA experience and the fact that those three guys were so cocky, they weren't afraid of anyone. That carried over to the rest of the team.

Going into the 1985 tournament, we thought our hardest game was going to be against the University of Dayton at Dayton in the first round. To play somebody on their home court in the NCAA Tournament can be tough. Sure enough, that was a difficult game. There was no shot clock, so the Flyers were holding the ball for the last shot with 40 seconds to go. If they ended up getting that last shot, this story wouldn't be in this book. Instead, we got a steal and Harold Jensen made a layup at the buzzer for the 51-49 win.

Even though that game figured to be our toughest, or scariest, and we won, we weren't thinking about winning the championship. In fact, there was never a point in the tournament where we started to think we had a good shot to win the tournament. It sounds like a cliché, but we really did take things one game at a time. When we beat North Carolina, the No. 2 seed, in the regional finals, then maybe there was a little glimmer of a light toward the end, but it still didn't seem possible. Our head coach, Rollie Massimino, had taken teams to the Elite Eight on three occasions before 1985, and knew the disappointment that a team faces when losing that regional final game. At no point did we think that we were going to win the championship, because we were too busy worrying about the task at hand.

When we finally did reach the championship game, we were facing a Big East Conference rival in Georgetown. In a strange way, it may have been lucky for us that we were playing the Hoyas. The "awe factor" was gone. Pinckney had big games against Georgetown's Patrick Ewing. As a team, we had good games against Georgetown. The Wildcats had defeated the Hoyas at Georgetown during the previous season on a last-second shot.

There's no question that the favored team in a championship game like that would much rather play a team that is not in its conference, because the advantage of the awe factor is gone. For the NCAA title game, that's a big bonus in our favor. There are a lot of teams in this country that were more talented than we were in 1985 that would have been intimidated playing against the Hoyas. Georgetown had been the best team in the country for two years, so it would be natural to be in awe of them. But, as a player, there's no point in being scared of them if you've played against them at least twice a year for your entire collegiate career.

Pinckney, for instance, had gone against the Hoyas at least eight other times before that title game, since arriving at Villanova. When he was a sophomore, Villanova played Georgetown at the Palestra and he had 26 points and 22 rebounds against Ewing. Before that title game everybody was talking about Ewing, Ewing, Ewing ... hey, Eddie Pinckney also was a pretty good college player.

Ewing was not a great offensive center in college. He dominated on the defensive end of the court. Offensively, the Hoyas spread the ball between Ewing, David Wingate, Bill Martin and Michael Jackson, instead of letting one guy dominate.

Even though they were a big favorite in that championship game, we knew we had a chance to beat them. We weren't necessarily going to go out and beat Georgetown that night; but, if we lost it wasn't going to be due to the fact that we were nervous or afraid to play that team. They might have beaten us for the simple fact that overall they were a better team.

Our players were ready to play. Coach Massimino was a master of game preparation. His gameplans were almost diabolical in that he thrived on finding a way to confuse opponents. He loved that. Every opponent he looked at, he saw from that angle. How can we get the opponent to do something that we want them to do, while making them think they're doing the right thing? That was his whole philosophy.

That's why he was so tough on teams that never saw Villanova. Just like we had a familiarity with Georgetown, it had one with us, too. The Hoyas didn't let the matchups bother them. To teams that didn't see us a lot, like Memphis State and Maryland, both of which we beat in that tournament, Coach was tough. All of his game plans against Georgetown were good, but we happened to shoot 79 percent from the field in this one, which helped.

The fact that the Wildcats put on a shooting clinic in the championship game, and how they did it, is beyond comprehension. What makes a team play its absolute best game ever, under the most difficult, pressure-packed situation? That says quite a bit about the guys on that 1985 Villanova team.

The two keys for us against Georgetown in the title, besides our shooting, were the tempo and the play of Villanova guard Gary McLain. Georgetown was a great full-court, man-to-man pressure defense team. McLain did a very good job of handling their pressure for 40 minutes. The game also was slow, which is what we wanted, because there was no shot clock; so we could be selective with our shots and literally play a half-court game against Georgetown.

Our game plan the entire time was to make the Hoyas play a half-court game, and hopefully be close enough to steal the game from them at the end. That's exactly what we did. Our guys did a wonderful job.

We had four players on the All-Tournament team, including Pinckney (Most Outstanding Player), McClain, McLain and Harold Jensen, who didn't even have that good of a regular-season, but at the end of the year he was incredible. Jensen is another case of a guy who, if you had told him in January that he was going to be on the All-Tournament team that season after Villanova won the national championship, would have thought you were crazy.

There is no way our team could have played better than it did that night. Let's look at it this way ... we shot 79 percent and won the championship game by two points, 66-64. What else could we do? How good were the Hoyas that we had to do all of that to beat them by two points!

When I look back at the 1985 title, it's a surreal experience because there was so much going on and so much emotion. Was I really there? Did it really happen? Everything went by so fast for me. It's really hard to put a finger on any one feeling that I could have had along the way. Heck, the year before, I was a 30-year-old high school coach, then all of a sudden I land the job at Villanova, and go on this incredible ride with the Wildcats in my first year. It seems nuts.

For me, having been to the championship game and knowing how the experience feels, helps me tell our kids that crazy things can happen. Somebody has to win the tournament, and it's not always the best teams or the best players who collect that ring. Hopefully I can make our guys believe in the possibility.

We haven't had that kind of success in the NCAA Tournament, but having been there in 1985 keeps me going with the thought that maybe this is our year. I still get chills each year when I watch the Final Four, but I also get upset because it's been 15 years since we were in that championship game. When I was the head coach at Manhattan in 1988, I talked about Villanova's title win all of the time. Now I can't talk about it because the kids we're recruiting were barely born in 1985.

On a road trip to play the University of Massachusetts during the 1999-2000 season, we took a field trip to the Basketball Hall of Fame. They have different video clips of championship games. Sure enough, there was the clip from the end of the 1985 game with me hugging Coach Mas at the end of the game. That's a famous clip. It's definitely a famous clip for me that will be in my mind forever.

You know, the championship ring that I have is priceless. A lot of things could be taken away from me, but they can't take that ring. It seems like people have tried though, by saying that if we played the Hoyas again, they would probably beat us. That might be true, but who cares how many times Georgetown would have beaten us in a series of games in 1985? I hope this experience happens to me again someday. I wouldn't mind playing a team that beats us 99-out-of-100 times. As long as our one win is in the national championship, nothing else matters.

As a high school coach at Truman High School in the Bronx in 1984, our team won the state championship. Then, in 1985, Villanova won the national championship. I probably should have retired after that, because everything had to be downhill following that two-year stretch.

CHAPTER 15

New Orleans, Louisiana
March 28 & 30, 1987

When the 3-point shot was introduced to college basketball before the 1986-1987 season, several players throughout the NCAA started licking their chops like a Doberman going after a piece of fresh meat. One of the most prolific outside shooters was Indiana Hoosier senior Steve Alford. Over the course of the season, Alford hit an incredible 53 percent of his 3-pointers (107-202).

Alford helped lead the Hoosiers to the 1987 title game in New Orleans against the upset-minded Syracuse Orangemen, coached by Jim Boeheim. In that title game, Alford hit an amazing seven 3-pointers in 10 attempts. He is tied for second with seven threes in a Final Four game behind the record of 10 set by UNLV's Freddie Banks, ironically, in the 1987 semifinals against Alford and the Hoosiers.

Boeheim's first trip to the NCAA Tournament came in 1966 as a player with Syracuse, where, in two tournament games, he scored 29 points. His first trip as the head coach of his alma mater, was in 1987 with a team that had a surprisingly good season. Nine years later, in 1996, Boeheim once again led the Orangemen to the Final Four, where they were defeated by Kentucky.

Indiana's 74-73 win over Syracuse in the 1987 title game will forever be marked by, what many consider, an unlikely hero ... Keith Smart. With five-seconds remaining in the game, Smart hit a 16-foot jumpshot to give the Hoosiers the victory ... a shot that Boeheim says he will never forget.

Today, Jim Boeheim continues to lead the Syracuse Orangemen, while Steve Alford is living what he considers his dream job, as the head basketball coach of the Iowa Hawkeyes.

 **Final Four Fast Facts** 1976 was the first year that two undefeated teams reached the Final Four — Indiana and Rutgers.

1987 All-Tournament Team

Steve Alford, Indiana
Derrick Coleman, Syracuse
Sherman Douglas, Syracuse
Armon Gilliam, UNLV
Keith Smart, Indiana
　(Most Outstanding Player)

Final Four Participants

Indiana
Providence
Syracuse
UNLV

National Semifinals

Indiana 97, UNLV 93
Syracuse 77, Providence 63

National Championship

Indiana 74, Syracuse 73

Steve Alford

The 1987 NCAA championship game against Syracuse was going to be a finalization of what a very exciting career for me at Indiana. It was nice to be playing on the last day that the NCAA allowed teams to play that season. I knew that regardless of what happened, my last game as a collegiate player was going to be in the championship game, in my first trip to the Final Four.

I will never forget that tremendous experience, with all of the fans and the entire hype of the whole event. The atmosphere is like that of a heavyweight boxing match. Being involved with that atmosphere, that hype, is a neat feeling.

We finished the season with a record of 30-4 and won the Big Ten championship, so it was a very positive year. Our resilient group of players that year was led on the sidelines by head coach Bob Knight, who was a tremendous coach. He did an incredible job of preparing us night-in and night-out. We always felt like we were the best-prepared team of the two that were playing.

Everybody talks about Coach Knight being worth about eight points on the sidelines. As a team we felt that we had that big of an advantage from a coaching standpoint, in every game.

I try to take those things that I learned from Coach Knight such as how to prepare for teams, how to break-down game tapes, how to utilize a walk-through ... basically how to set up my team for battle each night, and apply them to my coaching.

1987 Final, Indiana vs. Syracuse

Right now, as I'm living my dream job at the University of Iowa, I can hopefully take my experiences of playing for Coach Knight, and the success we had at Indiana, and develop the Hawkeye program similarly. The overall experience of playing in the Final Four, for instance, is an experience which I can apply to my coaching. Now I know what the atmosphere is like, and the feeling associated with, going that far in the tournament. Not only does it help in tournament situations, but it also helps in recruiting. Going into it, prospective players know that I have been involved in the championship game, and I'm working awfully hard now to get back there.

We made it to the 1987 championship game against Syracuse after a couple of close calls in the tournament. One of the closest was in the regional finals with Louisiana State University. Actually, we were beat against LSU. They had to miss some free throws and we had to make some big plays. Fortunately both things happened and we were able to pull out the 77-76 win on a Rick Calloway tip-in at the buzzer.

The title game with Syracuse went back and forth during the first half, with us leading 34-33 at halftime. The Orangemen built a decent lead and took over for most of the second half. We cut the lead in the last 10 minutes of the game, then Keith Smart had an incredible last five minutes.

I was pleased with the outcome of my performance, especially considering it was my final game, scoring 23 points and doing some nice things on both ends of the court. However, that game was really decided because of what Keith did in the last five minutes. He took over the game, scoring 12 of our team's last 15 points.

With a few seconds left in the game, Syracuse's Derrick Coleman was fouled and went to the line. A timeout was called

In 1978 Bob Bender became the only player in NCAA history to play for two different teams in the championship game ... he was a member of Indiana's 1976 undefeated team, and the 1978 Duke national runner-up team.

before he shot his free throws. We knew that we were going to have a chance to at least tie the game.

Obviously everybody knew their role on our team, and I was going to get a look on our next possession, but when we took the floor out of that timeout, we had confidence in any of our guys taking the final shot. We didn't know who was going to have the best chance of getting it, but we did know that once Coleman shot his free throws, make or miss, we were going to push the ball up the court for the last shot without calling a timeout.

When we brought the ball across the time line, Smart passed to

Daryl Thomas who couldn't get a shot, so he passed it back to Keith on the baseline. With five seconds left, Smart drained the 16-foot jumper for the 74-73 win and national championship.

In a situation with us trailing by a point, coming down the court with a few seconds on the clock and a chance to win, there really wasn't a main outlet, or player, expected to shoot the ball. We were confident in everybody's ability on the court. Up until the championship game, four of the five starters had their hand on a last-second shot to win a ballgame. Dean Garrett had a tip-in at the buzzer at Wisconsin; I made a last-second shot at Michigan; and Calloway tipped-in that missed shot by Thomas at the horn in the regional finals against LSU. The only other starter not involved (yet) was Keith Smart. It was only fitting that he hit the last-second basket in the final game of the season.

Different title teams have different stamps, but when people look at the stamp for our 1987 Indiana team ... we weren't the most athletic or talented team that has ever won a championship, but we rank up there with being one of the most resilient. We did a very good job of putting ourselves in a position to win with five minutes left in a game. Very seldom did we lose when we were leading with less than five minutes remaining. The only time we did lose under those circumstances that season, was to Illinois at Illinois. Overall, we just did a really nice job in the closing minutes of ballgames. In the championship game, Smart was largely responsible for helping us stay in position for the win.

Keith was simply incredible in the last five minutes against Syracuse. There aren't a lot of times when you can focus on one individual who took over a game, but Keith took control of this one. He was tremendous during that stretch, which was a key stretch to the game and our season. Then, for him to make the last shot was fitting because it solidified his dominance in the last few minutes of the championship game.

Jim Boeheim

The amount of time left in the 1987 championship game after Indiana's Keith Smart hit what turned out to be the game-winning shot, and if there was enough time or not for us to call a timeout, has been so blown out of proportion since that night. I have seen where some people have said there was as much as eight seconds left when he made the shot. In actuality, there were four seconds when the ball went into the basket, and we got it with two seconds left.

One of our players did signal for a timeout, and even though one of the referees did see it, the call wasn't real clear. Getting that timeout was not real important. It wasn't a situation where we had two timeouts and enough time to throw the ball to half-court and call another timeout. We did that when we played Georgia in the 1996 regional semifinals. In that game there were five seconds left, we threw it to half-court and called a timeout. Then we were able to set up a half-court play and won the ballgame. We only had one timeout against Indiana, so we couldn't do that.

Whether it would have been four seconds or two seconds, as actually was the case, it wouldn't have mattered because we still would have tried a long pass. Either way, one of the Hoosiers intercepted the pass. There aren't a ton of options with one timeout and two seconds left in the game when you have to go the length of the court.

We played about as well as we had played all year in that championship game, with a fairly young team. We did have two seniors, but we also had two freshmen and two sophomores that played quite a bit. Our Syracuse team was not what many would consider to be a Final Four team. It was a little of a surprise, but looking back at the players, we had very talented kids even though they were young. Because of that it's not a surprise that we played that well.

One of our main players on the 1986 team, Pearl Washington, left school early to enter the National Basketball Association draft. We were left with trying to find players to step up. Derrick Coleman was a freshman. Sophomore Sherman Douglas hadn't played much. Rony Seikaly was a pretty good junior. Then we had the two solid seniors, Greg Monroe and Howard Triche. Nobody had huge expectations for us that year.

We played pretty well all season, but we played great in the tournament starting with the Regional Finals against North Carolina. Going into that game, the Tar Heels were the No. 1 team in the nation, and we beat them by four points.

Against the Hoosiers, we had ourselves in position to win the ballgame, but Indiana made a couple of tough shots down the stretch to beat us. We had control of the scoreboard through most of the game, but it was pretty close. At one time in the second half we had an eight-point lead. We had a little bit more of an edge, particularly in the last 10-12 minutes of the game, but it was not out of reach. Keith Smart made sure of that.

Keith made not only the game-winning basket, but also five of the Hoosiers' other last six buckets. He was the only guy we couldn't stop. Down the stretch we kind of controlled Steve Alford and Indiana's inside people, but we just couldn't do anything with Smart. Up by one point, we had a one-and-one free throw situation with about 26 seconds to go with Coleman going to the line. A timeout was called.

During that timeout, we basically changed our defense to set up a junk defense of a triangle-and-two, since the Hoosiers had picked on our man-to-man defense. At that stage of the game, Smart had been the guy hurting us, so we were trying to make sure we guarded him and Alford. Overall we hadn't been a real good free throw shooting team, plus with Coleman being a freshman there was a lot of pressure in that situation. So our main concern was salvaging our lead.

Derrick missed the front end of the one-and-one, and Indiana got the rebound. On the ensuing play, our defense did a good job holding the Hoosiers until, with five seconds remaining, Smart got off a 16-foot shot from near the corner. It was a very tough shot, but he hit it for the 74-73 Indiana win. Obviously we didn't do a good enough job with our defense.

As a freshman, Coleman had an unbelievable game and season. Really, by any player's standards, Derrick was great with his 19 rebounds against Indiana. He was a monster on the boards. He came up huge in the game. He was dominant on the backboards during the whole night.

Jack "Goose" Givens' 41-point outpouring in the 1978 finals ranks seventh all-time for total points in a single Final Four game.

Derrick had nearly the same type of game against North Carolina in the Regional Finals, when he had 19 rebounds. With the Carolina and Indiana games, he had two unbelievable monster games, especially for a freshman.

Douglas had a great NCAA Tournament and a great game against Indiana, leading our scorers with 20 points and seven assists.

The whole Syracuse team played great. The championship game with Indiana was just a very good basketball game. I thought both teams played very well. They shot the hell out of the three-pointer, at least Alford did with seven, and we had some big plays. It was a great game to see. As a coach you obviously feel bad when you lose a game like that, but I don't think there was much that we could have done differently or better. We played well enough to win in our first trip to the Final Four.

There is no way to downplay going to the Final Four, especially as the head coach of my alma mater. The college game is all about being able to get there, and to play well once you do get there. We played well against Providence in the semifinals to get to the championship, then we played great against Indiana. College basketball is all about that final round. The first trip there is a tremendous experience and a tremendous thrill. I won't forget going to the Final Four in 1987. I won't forget the ending, either.

CHAPTER 16

Kansas City, Missouri
April 2 & 4, 1988

The 50th anniversary for the NCAA championship was awarded as a gift to Kansas City in the form of being able to host the Final Four. From 1940 through 1964, Kansas City's famed Municipal Auditorium had hosted more tournament games, 83, than any other arena, plus more national championship games, nine, than any other venue. Through the years, fans at Municipal had witnessed such incredible moments as North Carolina's triple-overtime championship win over Wilt Chamberlain and the Kansas Jayhawks in 1957; and UCLA coach John Wooden's first NCAA title in 1964. The city was about to receive another memorable experience in 1988.

With a season seemingly spoiled with injuries and academic problems, the Kansas Jayhawks, who had reached the Final Four in 1986, appeared to be headed for the National Invitational Tournament (that "other" postseason tournament) – especially with 11 losses under their belt. However, the team featuring senior Danny Manning was invited to the "Big Dance" as a sixth-seed at-large team. After an incredible run through the NCAA Tournament, the Jayhawks landed in their backyard — Kansas City's Kemper Arena — for the Final Four.

The other three teams in the Final Four were expected to be there. All three had automatically qualified for the tournament. Arizona and Oklahoma were top seeds in their regions. Duke, the team that defeated Kansas in the 1986 Final Four, was a No. 2 seed.

Even though it may not have been a dream match-up for the rest of the country, Big Eight fans in the Midwest were treated to a championship game with two of their representatives, Oklahoma and Kansas.

Billy Tubbs, who was the head coach of the Oklahoma team, appeared to be headed for his first national title. After all, his Sooners had defeated the Jayhawks twice in that 1987-1988 season. The voice of the Jayhawks, Bob Davis, who started with the team in 1986, had seen the arsenal that OU unloaded on teams. But, as he says, "Maybe the stars were aligned for the Jayhawks." Maybe.

1988 All-Tournament Team

Sean Elliott, Arizona
Stacey King, Oklahoma
Danny Manning, Kansas
  (Most Outstanding Player)
Milt Newton, Kansas
Dave Sieger, Oklahoma

Final Four Participants

Arizona
Duke
Kansas
Oklahoma

National Semifinals

Kansas 66, Duke 59
Oklahoma 86, Arizona 78

National Championship

Kansas 83, Oklahoma 79

Billy Tubbs

Probably the most vivid thing to me from the 1988 championship game against the Kansas Jayhawks, was losing. That's really about all. I do know that from the turn around of beating Arizona in the semifinals, to playing Kansas, was a real crowded time for us. By the time we did press conferences and interviews and met all of our obligations, it was a cram-packed time. There seemed to be little time to get ready to play a basketball game. Of course, Kansas had the same situation, so I'm not using that as an excuse. I just remember that as a crowded couple of days.

Thinking back, it was unusual because as a coach you always dream of getting into the finals of the NCAA, playing on a neutral court against a team you haven't seen all year. Instead, for us, it was a situation where we were playing a team we had played (and beaten) twice already, in the same building where we played our conference tournament a couple weeks prior. We were certainly excited about being there, but by the time teams get to that particular point in the season, there are a bunch of tired people involved.

Beating a team twice during the regular season, as we had with the Jayhawks, can work to that team's disadvantage. In the title game it worked against us. I don't think we were as excited about playing as we should have been. It's similar to the situation we frequently see in conference tournaments where a team is playing somebody that they've beaten twice in the year, and it's really hard to get excited about playing them again. I've experienced that a bunch of times going into conference tournaments. Half the time you end up getting beat. I would say that Kansas was probably a little more fired up to play us than we were to play them.

Don't get me wrong, this was a great Oklahoma team, talented enough that emotion maybe shouldn't have mattered. The chemistry of that team had been the key to our success in 1988. Once the group in 1987 lost to Iowa in the Regional Semifinals in overtime, the returning players vowed to get to the Final Four in 1988. They had set their sights on being in that championship game long before the season started. I don't even know if we were rated in the Top 25 to start 1987-1988, and we had fewer national television games than we had in any of the previous three or four years at Oklahoma; so I think that group was on a mission – with a cause. They were, by far, the best pressing team that I've ever had in my years of coaching. They could go out and create a lot of turnovers. They really played well together. I knew in November of 1987, during practice times, that it was going to be a special team. Indeed it was. We may have had a similar team in 1990, that was ranked No. 1 in the sportswriter's polls, but we probably had a more talented team overall in 1988.

We didn't necessarily approach the championship game with Kansas, or prepare, any differently than normal. We never really approached games differently, whether we had beaten a team twice already, or lost twice to them. When teams are playing in the NCAA Tournament, they don't really have time to do anything special. Again, we were playing a team with which we were pretty familiar. It wasn't like either one of us needed a lot time to prepare. Regardless, at that time of the season, when you get that far, you don't make a lot of grand or different preparations for any team. Time between opponents does not allow for big changes.

Our game plan, and hope, throughout that entire season was to have teams run with us. We didn't want people to hold the ball. That Oklahoma team was athletic, quick and could score some points. In fact, during the 1988 season, we were second in scoring average in the nation with 102.9 points a game. (Loyola Marymount averaged 110.3 points per game.) We felt that we could score when we needed to, and eventually wear the other team down. So, we were glad the Jayhawks ran with us in the first half of the championship game. I think the Jayhawks were a bit more surprised that they ran with us than we were. (Although Larry Brown [Kansas' head coach] would have to answer that.) They took some shots that we normally didn't see them taking. They were really hot and they made their baskets. The first half of that game, a lot of people think, was one of the greatest first halves of a championship game. It was a heck of first half, with the score tied, 50-50.

During halftime we made our normal adjustments. The first half was a typical Sooner half, but again, Kansas had played a great first half. We felt they couldn't, or wouldn't, play as well for the rest of the game. As it turned out, they played just as well in the second half, and we didn't. Unfortunately for us, the two teams went in completely opposite directions.

Two of the main players who helped us in that championship game, especially in the first half, were Mookie Blaylock and Dave Sieger. Blaylock had seven steals in the game, and Sieger hit seven three-pointers.

Blaylock has always been a fun player to watch. He is certainly quick, maybe not the quickest I've coached, but he's the best I've ever coached at just stripping the ball from somebody; just taking it away from them on the dribble. His speed and quickness were good but his anticipation was much better. Mookie knew how to set up a guy and then clean him. At one time he held the record for steals in a game with 13.

I remember hearing an interview with one of the Kansas guards, a year or two after the championship game, and he said that playing against the Oklahoma guards was a nightmare, with the pressure and harassment defensively that they would give opponents. When I hear that kind of comment, unsolicited, on a radio show, that's a pretty nice compliment for our kids like Mookie.

As for Sieger, he had a great game and just an outstanding first half against Milt Newton of Kansas. Dave hit six of the eight threes he launched. Too bad we couldn't have continued that play into the second half. He had a big first half, with almost 20 points.

Two of our inside players who normally came up big for us, Stacey King and Harvey Grant, had off-games against Danny Manning and Kansas in the championship. It was not their best performance, but they were solid. Manning was a key for Kansas that night. He was a great player and he had a great game against us, scoring 31 points and grabbing 18 rebounds. We didn't shut Manning down and neither one of our big guys had what you would even call their average game against him.

One thing that somewhat broke down our strategy and some things that we wanted to do, was that Kansas had Manning handling the ball, bringing it down the floor against our pressure. Our big guys hadn't had to go out top to defend against people bringing the ball down the court, and we got into some mismatches because of that. Manning probably helped Kansas more with bringing the ball down a few times than anything else he did in the game. That really made us get out of our pressing defenses. But, all in all, their whole team just had an unbelievable game. It was just their night.

Usually the thing that made Danny a great player was the fact that he shot the ball so well. He could face up to the basket and knock a shot down; or, he could post up and knock it down. But then in the championship game, he handled the ball better than we expected. When we played against Manning, we didn't necessarily feel like we had to shut him down offensively to win, but certainly it would have helped. I don't know if there was any way to stop him in the title game. We even tried to double-team him a couple times, leaving other Kansas players wide open. Chris Piper made us pay for that one time. He only had eight points in the game, but he hit a critical basket late in the game when we weren't guarding him. Then, with five seconds left in the game, Manning sealed the Jayhawk win, hitting two free throws. Final score, Kansas won 83-79.

The one thing that I remember about that 1988 championship game is that it wasn't a bad game. People might say that we weren't ready to play, we didn't care, or any of that other stuff that is sometimes said. I have no regrets about the way my team played. We didn't play absolutely horrendous, or like we didn't care and therefore went out there and blew the game. It wasn't like there were a lot of turnovers and we were lousy. Our guys gave a great effort and we played pretty well. I just felt that Kansas had an exceptional game; a heck of a game. After it was over, I was sorry that we lost, but I don't look back and have a lot of regrets about that game because of the fact that if you give a great

Final Four Fast Facts

In 1978, Jim Spanarkel (20/21), Mike Gminski (29/20) and Gene Banks (22/22) became the only threesome to score at least 20 points in both Final Four games.

effort, which I thought our team in general did, there is nothing to be ashamed about. There are a lot of plays we would like to replay, but I never missed a lot of sleep over that championship game.

1988 Final, Kansas vs. Oklahoma

Bob Davis

Going to the Final Four is the ultimate in college basketball. I've been fortunate to go four times as the University of Kansas broadcaster. I've also broadcast several women's Final Fours for the NCAA. You never lose the thrill of going to the championship round. It is unique each time you go. The Final Four has become such a colossal event, right up there with the World Series and Super Bowl ... it's perhaps the ultimate in college sports. For me it's been a great thrill to be with a team that reaches that level.

Head coach Larry Brown led the program to the Final Four in 1986, my second year with the Jayhawks, and in 1988; then we've been twice, so far, with Roy Williams, 1991 and 1993. Kansas has had five coaches get to a Final Four, and I've been lucky enough to go with two of them. Larry's Kansas teams were picked by many to reach the Final Four before the season began each of those years. Roy did it with a couple of squads that were surprises to get that far.

Any team that gets to a Final Four has had a sensational season, or at least a remarkable run at tournament time. Of course it's even better to win the championship. To win four straight NCAA Tournament ballgames under that type of pressure and competition just to reach the Final Four, is amazing.

The first time I went as a broadcaster was in 1986, with a Kansas team that probably expected to be there from day one. That was a senior team that had returned all five starters, including sophomore Danny Manning. They went 13-1 in the Big Eight Conference, and had a super year. Unfortunately, Archie Marshall blew out a knee in the semifinal game against Duke, then the team got into foul trouble. Marshall was a player who was destined for stardom in college and perhaps in a NBA career.

Had the Jayhawks defeated the Blue Devils in that 1986 semifinal game, I would have liked their chances on Monday night against Louisville because Kansas had defeated the Cardinals twice during the regular season that year. But, I guess the Oklahoma title game of 1988 proves that you don't always win that third game.

The 1988 Final Four was unique because, for one thing, it was in Kansas City, it was the 50th Anniversary of the Final Four and the half-time score of the championship game was 50-50. All the stars seemed to be aligned.

When we started that season, Kansas had great hopes of being in the Final Four. Those hopes seemed to be squelched throughout the early part of the year with some injuries and academic problems. One of the biggest blows to the team was the loss of Marshall, who was a fan favorite. Archie blew out the ACL in one of his knees in 1986, missed the next season, then he blew out his other ACL during the 1988 season.

After their 20th game of the year, the Jayhawks had a record of 12-8, and were on a four-game losing streak, two of which were at home in Lawrence. There were probably some fans out there thinking about the possibility of the National Invitational Tournament (NIT) instead of the NCAA Tournament. The Jayhawks did have the best player in college basketball that year, Manning, and as long as he was healthy, anything was possible.

Danny came out of Lawrence High School, located in the shadows of the KU campus, as one of the two most highly regarded prospects in the country. Sometimes players who come out as the most heralded don't reach all of that fanfare throughout their careers. Manning did, and more. He carried that burden from day one.

As a freshman and sophomore, Danny was such a terrific team player. On the 1986 Final Four team, Manning was surrounded by veteran seniors like Ron Kellogg, Greg Dreiling and Calvin Thompson. Manning did a great job of playing up to those guys. He was a good assist man who helped make the other guys around him better. By the time Danny was a senior, Larry Brown told him that it was not a democracy... Manning had to really take control of the team. He certainly did, leading them to the national championship. Even though he was taking control of the team, he still managed to make everyone around him better players.

Larry Brown was really an interesting guy. He was about as good a bench coach as anybody in the sport. He was a great technician and had a great feel for his personnel; he could make great adjustments during the game. (Of course it doesn't hurt to have a player like Manning around whom Larry could build the team.)

Brown was a great coach. He took UCLA to a Final Four in just two years, then he took two KU teams to the Final Four in five years. He's been pretty remarkable. It has been a little different for him at the professional level, but he's done well where he has been. Despite not winning a NBA championship, he has taken organizations that needed to be built, and built them into playoff-caliber teams. He is certainly one of the true great basketball coaches in the country.

The Jayhawks, with a record of 21-11, received an at-large berth in the 1988 NCAA Tournament. The tightest game for Kansas was in the second round against Murray State. The Racers' guard put up a last-second shot that would have won the game for them, but Danny got a piece of the ball and deflected it. During the battle for the ensuing rebound, Danny was fouled, and made a couple of free throws to give the Jayhawks a 61-58 win.

A lot of things throughout that tournament helped sixth-seeded KU. North Carolina State got upset in the first round of the tournament by Murray State. Vanderbilt upset Pittsburgh in the second round. When we went to Pontiac, Mich., for the regionals, the four teams were Kansas, Kansas State, Purdue and Vanderbilt. The Jayhawks and Vanderbilt (seventh-seed) were, needless to say, not expected to be in Pontiac.

Everybody was picking that great Purdue team for the Final Four. But, I can confidently say that the 1988 K-State team was one of the greatest Wildcat squads of all time, highlighted by the play of Mitch Richmond.

If Kansas and Kansas State each won their games, the two teams would meet in the regional finals. One of my big memories of the whole tournament was the regional semifinal night with over 30,000 people in the Silverdome. The K-State people were cheering for KU in their game with Vanderbilt; and likewise, the KU people were cheering for K-State against Purdue. Lo and behold, both Kansas teams won!

Kansas and Kansas State played on that Sunday afternoon in a colossal game. It was the first time the two programs had ever played each other away from Lawrence, Manhattan or Kansas City, in arguably the biggest game of all time between the two programs. It was not only a great game, but it was a situation where one of the two teams was going to the Final Four. Talk about bragging rights in the state of Kansas! There was quite a bit on the line. Needless to say, the Jayhawks went on to win the game, 71-58.

The K-State coach at the time, Lon Kruger, whom I have always admired and liked, handled that loss with as much class and dignity as anybody possibly could in what had to have been such a stinging loss. He did well at K-State, then got Florida to the Final Four, and it looks like he's going to have a heck of a run at the University of Illinois. I wish him nothing but the best of luck.

With that win over K-State, the Jayhawks had earned another trip to the Final Four. Oddly, they were going to have a chance to avenge their 1986 semifinal loss, and an earlier 1988 loss in Lawrence, facing the Duke Blue Devils. Duke had earned a trip to the Final Four by beating the No. 1 team in the nation, Temple. In the first half of the 1988 semifinal game, Manning led the Jayhawks with 15 points, followed by Milt Newton with 14, as KU led Duke at the break, 38-27. The Jayhawks held off a couple of big Duke runs in the second half, and won, 66-59. The Jayhawks were going to the championship game for the first time since

1957! As the rest of the night unfolded, Oklahoma helped stage an all-Big Eight final by knocking off Arizona in the other semifinal game, 86-78.

Even though the Jayhawks had lost to the Sooners twice in the season, they competed pretty well in both games. I don't think they were in awe of Oklahoma, although they knew the Sooners had a very good ballclub. Sometimes in the back of your head, if you think you're playing well and have a good team, you don't think a team can beat you three times. On the other side, however, Oklahoma felt like they could be at Kansas three times that season, and maybe rightly so, because they were loaded, including four future NBA players.

A lot of people thought KU would have to slow down the tempo of the championship game against the quick, high-scoring Oklahoma Sooners. Instead, the Jayhawks proved they could run with Oklahoma. One key to being able to run was that Kansas went deeper into its bench and played more players in the game. The Sooners only played six players, whereas 10 Jayhawks saw action in the title game. Maybe because of that, the KU players were a little fresher in the second half.

Fittingly, Danny was the key overall; he had a huge ballgame. The way he played in that game was phenomenal. But again, he made the people around him play better. Even taking away his game statistics of 31 points and 18 rebounds, the other guys shot close to 71 percent from the field. They really hit some big shots. Milt Newton was on fire in the first half with a couple of big three-pointers. Chris Piper hit a baseline basket as the shot clock expired. Clint Normore had a big three-pointer from the head of the circle. There were some plays like those that were very crucial for the Jayhawks in that game.

Luckily, some of those unheralded guys, like Newton, stepped in and played well throughout the season. Jeff Gueldner was a young player on that team, who became a starter and a good three-point shooter. Kevin Pritchard made the move to point guard and handled it well. Piper, who played most of that year with a groin injury, and therefore, with great courage, became one of the best defensive big men in college basketball. Former North Carolina coach Dean Smith said that Piper's fundamentals were close to perfect for a defensive player. The combination of that group, as well as the guys coming off the bench, really got the job done. Because of the injuries the team suffered early in the season, Danny felt, at first, he had to carry them, until some of the other guys stepped up.

Manning was the type of player who made things happen when the team needed a lift. He got the big rebounds, defended well, and did the things that people normally don't talk about. He also hit four big free throws down the stretch of the championship game that kept it out of reach. He was really a dominant player.

It was a tough break for OU, as it turned out, to have had to play the Jayhawks in Kansas City. Head coach Billy Tubbs never liked coming to Kansas City for the Big Eight Tournament. Then, for the Final Four, a great moment for him and his team, they have to play the Jayhawks in Kansas City. Maybe that's how everything was supposed to be.

The Kansas team was nicknamed, "Danny and the Miracles" ... obviously for a good reason. The Jayhawks pulled off the "upset" and beat the Oklahoma Sooners, 83-79, in an incredibly exciting championship game. Danny definitely played like the Player of the Year and the MVP of the Final Four. Who knows, maybe the 1988 Kansas team was one of destiny.

The last three losses the Jayhawks suffered during the season were to Duke, Oklahoma and Kansas State (in the Big Eight Tournament). The last three wins of the season for Kansas, interestingly enough, were against Kansas State (NCAA Tournament Midwest Regional Final), Duke and Oklahoma.

A couple of months after the remarkable 1988 championship, the Jayhawks were placed on NCAA probation for a recruiting violation, thus becoming the only national champion not given the opportunity to retain its title. I don't think the probation taints the championship team at all because the player involved in the violation had nothing to do with that team. In fact, that player never played at KU. A lot of innocent kids, guys who had come back for the 1989 season, had to pay quite a price for some-

Final Four Fast Facts

Michigan State is one of only two schools (Stanford, 1942) to have a losing record the season (1980) after it won the title.

thing in which they were not involved at all. Some innocent people were hurt. I guess that's how it works in college athletics sometimes.

Right before the NCAA investigation was announced, Larry moved on to the pros (San Antonio Spurs) and Kansas got Roy Williams, who had been trained by the master, Dean Smith, at North Carolina. Since then, Roy has become one of the master coaches in college basketball, and he did it in a relatively short amount of time. Two years after coming to Kansas, Roy was a 30 game winner; and three years after coming he was in the Final Four. He has won several conference championships, and has kept Kansas as one of the elite programs in the country.

In the long run, Kansas basketball has been in pretty good hands since 1988.

CHAPTER 17

Seattle, Washington
April 1 & 3, 1989

The 1989 championship game between Seton Hall and Michigan is considered by many to be one of the most exciting title games in tournament history, yet it seems to be one of the most forgotten ... or at least the final few seconds and their effect on basketball don't seem to be remembered.

With Seton Hall leading 79-78 in the final seconds of the game, referee John Clougherty called a block foul against the Pirates' Gerald Greene, thus sending Michigan's Rumeal Robinson to the free-throw line with no time left on the clock. The junior hit both shots from the charity stripe for the national championship.

The 1989 championship game not only featured two No. 3 seeds – the first time since seeding began in the 1970s that at least one No. 1 or No. 2 seeded team was in the final game – but it was the first time in history that a team won its semifinal and final games by a combined total of three or fewer points. The Wolverines defeated Illinois by two points and Seton Hall by one point.

Although he has worked nearly every Final Four since 1982, the 1989 championship game is one which is lodged into the memory bank of CBS broadcaster Tim Brando. From 1987-1990 Brando hosted ESPN's coverage of the NCAA Men's Basketball Championship. He stayed in the same Seattle hotel as Clougherty, and the two spoke briefly about the call later that night.

Brando joined CBS Sports in 1995, and currently is the studio host for *CBS' College Football Today*, as well as a play-by-play announcer for NFL and NCAA men's basketball games on the network.

 **Final Four Fast Facts** Kansas is the only program not given an opportunity to repeat as National Champions. They were placed on probation after the 1988 season. Larry Brown became the only coach to leave for another coaching job (the NBA's San Antonio Spurs) after his school won the title.

1989 All-Tournament Team	Final Four Participants
Danny Ferry, Duke	Duke
Gerald Greene, Seton Hall	Illinois
John Morton, Seton Hall	Michigan
Glen Rice, Michigan	Seton Hall
(Most Outstanding Player)	
Rumeal Robinson, Michigan	

National Semifinals	National Championship
Michigan 83, Illinois 81	Michigan 80, Seton Hall 79 (OT)
Seton Hall 95, Duke 78	

Tim Brando

Imagine the furor that would be caused by the unmitigated gall of an official to alter the outcome of the Super Bowl with a subjective pass interference call with just a few ticks remaining on the clock. Imagine the Stanley Cup decided by a penalty shot awarded in the final few seconds. Imagine if the finish of one of the best Final Four trio of games and the national title was predicated by a block/charge call with just a few seconds remaining.

The aforementioned circumstances seem almost impossible to fathom. In the world of sports, game officials always err to the side of leniency in the waning moments. The players, the coaches, the game officials all desire "clean closure."

In 1989, the NCAA men's championship scenario came to fruition with the game between the Seton Hall Pirates and Michigan Wolverines being decided in essence by the judgment of one of the most respected, admired and desired officials in the game. The game was decided by one of the most difficult and abstract rulings in sport ... that being the block/charge.

The game forever altered the "unwritten" laws game officials now abide by.

Keep in mind, few debated the call. Most agreed with the verdict. However, the fact the call was made with seconds remaining in an NCAA final left the masses with a collective case of drop-jaw and amplified the belief that a "swallowed whistle" is the best whistle when the game hangs in the balance.

While Michael Jordan's game-winning shot in the 1982 final gave North Carolina Coach Dean Smith his first national title is a memory chiseled into my mind, what I'll never forget about my first Final Four experience was the aura, the ambiance, the entire package. There were more than 60,000 eyewitnesses to the game inside the Superdome with both teams playing at a level rarely seen. The colors, the bands, the fans, and the electricity is what makes the Final Four so special.

I was hooked, and the Final Four memories stored since then are in abundance. There have been volumes of great plays, great players, great games, great coaches and great situations. However, the 1989 Final Four has a special corner in my gray matter.

Having called the game of basketball, having hosted the tournament from the studios of Bristol for ESPN, having developed a love for the game, I knew that the Final Four was special for many reasons. A new city, the travel, the food and, in 1989, taking my family made it a unique experience.

While watching the family in awe of the surroundings, I knew the two days of play would surely unravel a gem. It was a magnificent four-some chock full with story lines and enthusiasm.

Seton Hall's P.J. Carlesimo brought a cast from New Jersey, which had captured the underdog role and the fascination of the masses. A few years earlier, Pirates fans were ready to run P.J. out of town. He was finally about to enjoy the fruits of his labor in the greatest setting in sports.

Duke was becoming a staple in the Final Four as Coach Mike Krzyzewski's star was skyrocketing. The Blue Devils were making their third appearance in four years, yet were still looking to cut the net for the first time on Coach K's watch.

Michigan was the Cinderella story – overcoming tougher opposition off the court than on the court at times. Michigan Athletic Director Bo Schembechler had decided there was no way, "an Arizona State coach was going to lead a Michigan team into the tournament."

Hence, Coach Bill Frieder was dismissed to assume his duties at ASU, a job he accepted while expecting to lead the Wolves into the tournament. Assistant Steve Fisher would now take over. Fisher was an unknown commodity faced with an incredible task of preparing for his assignment all the while knowing it was unlikely he would retain control of the program after the tournament. With each victory, he ensured that the scenario would change. It was like the Wolverines were feeding off the negative energy for positive results.

Illinois offered a fabulous group of athletes capable of running with the best. It was a high-flying group that attacked offensively while smothering foes defensively. In Coach Lou Henson, making his second Final Four appearance after having led New Mexico State to the show 19 years before, Illinois had a perfect coaching complement for its personnel. The first two games didn't disappoint, with Michigan and Seton Hall surviving and scheduled to meet in the finals.

Little did I know as the Pirates and Wolverines battled for the opening tip, that this game would prove to be an embryonic event for the means in which the game is played and called for eternity.

For the first time – the public – the casual basketball fan would become intimate with the term block/charge. John Clougherty is one of the best officials I've had a chance to see work. He was an official seemingly always in control of the game, the players, and the coaches.

Clougherty was never content, he was always looking for input in order to improve "his game." He was an official I became so familiar with that I was even surprised at the intestinal fortitude he displayed in the waning seconds of overtime of an NCAA Final Four title game.

With the intensity and excitement level at optimum tones, Clougherty would blow his whistle, calling a blocking foul against the Pirates and sending Michigan's Rumeal Robinson to the free-throw line for the deciding points.

It was incredible that a block/charge call would decide one of the greatest games in NCAA history. The decision and outcome of the '89 Final changed the way the game would be officiated forever. On the largest stage imaginable, an official made the strongest move imaginable. He made the players accountable for their actions. Clougherty, a veteran of the game who hailed from Raleigh, N.C., decided the game should be called the same start to finish. What was good in the first few seconds ... was good for the last few seconds.

If you look back at the way the 1989 title game's final play evolved he made the proper call. In overtime, the first championship game extra frame since 1963, the Pirates were leading by one point with less than 10 seconds to play. Carlesimo appeared to have his championship. Michigan's Rumeal Robinson drove down the court toward a waiting Seton Hall defender. As he got in the lane, there was a collision. A blocking foul was called on the Pirates as time expired. Robinson, a 65 percent free throw shooter during the season, would have a chance to see if the glass slipper fit on the Wolverines' foot. It did.

By making the call, Clougherty proved his worth as an official. You don't get to call the gem game without the credentials. Many officials are so cognizant of the abstract that sometimes it alters their thought process. Clougherty was so focused that night he was able to show complete disregard for the circumstances and make the right call.

Carlesimo never took a shot at Clougherty because he made the right call. If you looked around the stadium that evening you saw a look of disbelief, but never did the masses question the call. It was the right call. But time would prove it was the right call at the wrong time.

From that point on, college officials adopted the NBA mindset ...

 **Final Four® Fast Facts** — Indiana State head coach, Bill Hodges, is one of only seven coaches who has guided his team to the Final Four in his first season as the head coach (1979).

they now swallow the whistle in the final moments when the game is tight, giving the players freedom not granted in the first 38-some minutes.

While Seattle provided a tremendous setting for the Final Four, while the trio of games offered numerous thrills a minute, my most memorable scene occurred after the game.

Having returned to the hotel nearly three hours after the game, I was surprised to see Clougherty standing alone in the lobby. His face wasn't recognizable to the masses; thus he leaned up against the wall quenching his thirst in anonymity.

With the wall supporting him, I approached with a great sense of sympathy. I knew, he knew, the fallout sure to the follow.

"Timmy, what did you think?" he asked. "Was it a good call?"

I said, "John, it was a good call, it was the only call you could make."

He shook his head in acceptance. He never spoke about the situation again.

So while the '89 Final Four was a perfect setting to catapult the event into the stratosphere in the '90s, for me it will always be remembered for the block/charge call, and a referee who had the inner-strength to make the right call at any time.

Part V: The '90s

CHAPTER 18

Indianapolis, Indiana
March 30 & April 1, 1991

The 1991 semifinal games featured two of the most intriguing match-ups that the Final Four had seen in several years. The early Saturday game featured Kansas against North Carolina. Roy Williams against Dean Smith. Student against teacher. The nightcap between Duke and UNLV was a rematch of the 1990 title game in which the Blue Devils suffered the biggest defeat in a NCAA championship game, 103-73.

This was a new season for Duke. One 30-point embarrassment in a championship game was one too many. The Blue Devils relaxed and had fun during the 1990-1991 season, and were set for another meeting with the Runnin' Rebels, a team considered by many to be unbeatable. And why not? UNLV had their nucleus back from the destructive national championship team.

Bob Harris has been the radio voice of the Duke Blue Devils for more than 25 years, which has included interviewing Duke head coach Mike Krzyzewski more than any other person. Like most Duke fans, Harris has lived through the disappointments of losing in four-out-of-five Final Fours before finally winning the school's first title in 1991.

Matching wits with Dean Smith is a nearly impossible task. However, Roy Williams, in his first trip to the Final Four as a head coach, may have nearly done that, as the No. 3-seeded Jayhawks knocked off the top-seeded Tar Heels to advance to the championship game against Duke. Williams has admitted that after his team won the first game of the night, deep down he may have been pulling for UNLV to win as expected over Duke because the Jayhawks matched up better with the Runnin' Rebels.

1991 All-Tournament Team

Anderson Hunt, UNLV
Bobby Hurley, Duke
Christian Laettner, Duke
  (Most Outstanding Player)
Bill McCaffrey, Duke
Mark Randall, Kansas

Final Four Participants

Duke
Kansas
North Carolina
UNLV

National Semifinals

Duke 79, UNLV 77
Kansas 79, North Carolina 73

National Championship

Duke 72, Kansas 65

Bob Harris

After a crushing defeat at the hands of UNLV in the 1990 NCAA championship game, 103-73, I think there was a sense of revenge for the Duke Blue Devils in the 1991 semifinals. Not only was that 1990 loss an embarrassment that rankled the Duke faithful for quite some time, it was the worst loss that any team had suffered in the NCAA championship game. When the team found out they were going to play UNLV in the 1991 semifinal game, the Duke coaching staff took a different tactical approach than they had the previous year.

Coach Mike Krzyzewski did one of the best psych jobs with the Rebels that I have ever seen. "From this point on, don't believe anything you hear except what I tell you in the locker room," he told his team in the locker room after the regional championship against St. John's. He then proceeded to do a snow job on UNLV coach Jerry Tarkanian, playing with the Runnin' Rebels' heads saying how great a team UNLV had, that it was almost an impossible task for Duke to go up against them, and other such comments. Watching Mike during that time was truly amazing.

Krzyzewski is one of the best at getting a team ready in a situation like that. He had five days to get ready for UNLV, which was a perfect amount of time. Even though the Rebels came into that game with an incredible 45-game unbeaten streak, the Blue Devils did a remarkable job of preparing. They were so focused on what they had to do to win.

The Duke kids were loose before that game. When I went to the locker room to tape Mike's pregame show during halftime of the day's first semifinal game, he was in a film session with guard Bobby Hurley. While I was waiting in the locker room and watching that Kansas-North Carolina game on television with most of the players, sportscaster Lesley Visser had gone down the hallway in front of the locker room to do her live report. One of the Duke players, Thomas Hill, got up and left the room. When somebody asked where he was going, a couple of guys said, "Shhh, just watch the TV." As Lesley was doing this live shot in front of a door, it suddenly opened and a man's head popped out with a waving hand. It was Hill. He came running back in and all the players started high-fiving and laughing. It was an unbelievable situation. This team was loose!

As I headed down the hallway after interviewing Krzyzewski, the UNLV bus pulled up. Watching the Rebels get off the bus it was obvious that they weren't having any fun at all. They were as tight as tight could be. They almost looked like a group of staunch Supreme Court justices.

Despite their stiff appearance, one thing that sticks out in my mind from the Duke-UNLV game was the confidence, to the point of cockiness, that the Runnin' Rebels displayed ... they didn't think anyone could beat them. Why should they? They had everybody back from their 1990 title team that cakewalked through the Final Four, including Larry Johnson, Stacey Augmon, Anderson Hunt and Greg Anthony.

That group of guys, along with their teammates, still has one of the largest scoring margins per game in a season in history, outscoring its opponents by nearly 27 points a contest. That is the biggest scoring difference since the 1972 UCLA team averaged the largest-ever at 30 points a game.

Don't get me wrong, we had confident players at Duke. The one player from that team who most people think about from the confidence category is probably Christian Laettner, who is a piece of work in a lot of ways. He is a bit arrogant and a bit brash, but a competitive basketball player with a lot of good basketball sense. He and Hurley were the two most competitive people I have ever been around. They would not lose

– they would do everything they could to find some way to beat you all the way until the final buzzer went off. They wouldn't quit.

In college Laettner pushed people as far as they would let him. He had that much kid in him. He just needed to be taken down a notch at times, and he respected people who did that. Laettner was the same with the younger players in that if they backed off from him, he had no respect for them, but if they got back in his face he loved it. It has always been so interesting to watch how these kids work together and how they develop relationships.

On the court, Laettner had that ability to make something happen when it needed to happen. There were very few times that he didn't come through in the clutch. One time he didn't however, was toward the end of a 1989 game with Arizona at the Meadowlands in New Jersey during his freshman season. He went to the free-throw line for two shots with 14 seconds left, and missed them. Duke lost 77-75.

After the game I was standing in the hallway outside of the Duke locker room with Wilt Browning, a writer from Greensboro. We were waiting on the locker room to open so I could do the postgame show. We heard footsteps coming around one of the long, curved hallways in the basement at the Meadowlands, and I turned to see who it was.

It was Richard Nixon.

We knew that he was at the game because we had seen him across the court. He came walking over to us by himself, without any type of security. When he got closer I introduced myself to him. He said, "You've got the best job in America, haven't you?" Naturally, I agreed.

President Nixon loved sports. He agreed to do an interview with us during the postgame show. Our engineer at that time was a staunch Democrat; believe me, we did not talk politics because he would get mad in a heartbeat. I got on the two-way radio and said, "Send it to me when this commercial is over."

He asked, "Is the locker room open?"

"No, but I've got Richard Nixon with me."

"So?"

I said, "We're going to interview him for postgame because he's a former president of the United States and a Duke Law School graduate. Do you need anything else?" After we chatted and did a postgame interview, the former president received permission to go into the Duke locker room. He went straight to Laettner and talked to him about the missed free throws. Nixon recognized the competitiveness, I think at that point, in Laettner.

The one thing everybody remembers Nixon telling Laettner is, "I've missed a few, too. Things will work out. There will be day that you'll make a shot like that that'll win a big game for Duke." (Was this fore-shadowing!)

Once the ball was tipped off in the 1991 semifinal game, it looked as though Coach K had a good game plan. Behind Laettner's hot shooting hand, and a stingy Blue Devil defense, Duke took an early lead. However, the defending national champs were too talented and cocky to sit back and watch their title slip away. Despite Anthony fouling out for UNLV with more than three minutes to play, the teams stayed close to each other. The game was tied 77-77 in the final seconds.

With 12.7 seconds left in regulation, Laettner hit two free throws on a one-and-one situation to give the Blue Devils a 79-77 lead. For him to hit those two shots in that situation took ice water in the veins. UNLV had the ball on the last possession with enough time left to win it, being down by two. They worked the ball around, but couldn't find the shot they wanted. Anderson Hunt threw up a desperation 25-foot three-pointer that missed at the buzzer. Duke won, 79-77. UNLV's Johnson, Augmon and Hunt each played 39 minutes in that contest, while Laettner and Hurley each played all 40 minutes.

Most people felt that the Duke-UNLV semifinal was the championship game even though the winner still had to prove itself one more time. The Blue Devils had to guard against thinking they had the title wrapped up by beating UNLV ... they still had to play Kansas for the actual title. When the buzzer sounded after the semifinal game, Krzyzewski was yelling to his players, "No celebrating yet. No celebrating yet." He did not want his team revelling at all because they had not won anything, except one game. Hurley was one of the players running off the floor with his index finger raised saying, "One more game," not "We're number one!" He was shouting that all the way to the locker room.

But, after defeating the Runnin' Rebels, a seemingly invincible team, it is easy to see why the Duke players felt like they could beat anyone. The Jayhawks may have felt a similar high after knocking off Indiana (ranked No. 3), Arkansas (No. 2 ranked) and North Carolina (ranked No. 4) to reach the finals, but they had expended a lot of energy in their semifinal game with the Tar Heels. That was Roy Williams, the student, against Dean Smith, the mentor. The game was one in which Smith was ejected after his second technical foul, and then-Carolina assistant coach Bill Guthridge went after the referee in the hallway.

Behind Laettner's 18 points, including a perfect 12-for-12 from the free-throw line, the Blue Devils had a relatively easy time beating Kansas, 72-65. Laettner captured Most Valuable Player honors for his play in the Final Four.

Stories From the Final Four: The '90s

There was a collective sigh of relief that Duke had finally won a National Championship. The fans felt the team probably deserved it in 1964 and 1986. Both of those years the Blue Devils clearly had the best team in the country. In 1991, Duke may not have had the best team in the country; UNLV may have been the best, but on one particular night they were not. The mark of a champion is the ability to win the big game, when you play the big game.

Everybody talked about how winning that first title was a way for Coach K to get the monkey off his back, but he always said, "I don't perceive it as having a monkey on the back by not winning a national championship. I consider it a mantle of excellence to even get to the Final Four as many times as we have (four straight). The hard part is getting there; the hard part isn't winning it."

The next season, Duke had another special team. In fact, that 1991-1992 team sticks out in my mind as much as any other because of what they did and how they did it. For a team in this day and age in college basketball to be ranked preseason No. 1, go through the season every week at No. 1, and finish No. 1 with a national championship, as the Blue Devils did, is truly amazing.

Duke finished the season with an overall record of 34-2. The two times the team lost during the season, the other top teams in the polls also lost. So, despite the two losses, the Blue Devils never dropped out of that top spot in the polls. During the first week of February, we lost at Carolina on a Wednesday night. Two of the top five teams lost that night, while the other three lost on Saturday. Virtually the same thing happened later in February when we lost at Wake Forest, and the two teams right below us lost. Both losses that season were on the road by a total of six points.

One of the biggest wins for the favored Blue Devils that season, if not the most memorable, was the heart-stopping East Regional Final game against Kentucky. A lot of people, myself included, think that was the greatest NCAA game of all time for what was accomplished and what was on the line. Regulation was draining enough, but to go into overtime and have a last-second shot was phenomenal.

The ebb and flow of that game was superb, with the momentum constantly switching back and forth. Each team looked like they were going to seize control of that momentum and win the game, but then the other team would make a run and come back.

With Duke leading 102-101 late in overtime, Kentucky's Sean Woods hit a soft shot over Laettner's head to put the Wildcats ahead. That basket forced Duke to call a timeout with 1.8 seconds remaining, trailing 103-102. The Kentucky fans knew they were going to the Final Four.

There was no way Duke was going to be able to go the length of the court, and score, in less than two seconds ... right?

We sent the broadcast to a commercial break, I leaned back in my chair, put my hands behind my head, looked up at the scoreboard and tried to figure out all of the possible scenarios, and who might take the shot for Duke. Basically I figured either Kentucky would win 103-102, or either Laettner, Hurley or Grant Hill would hit a shot and Duke would win 104-103. 104-103. 104-103. I said that over and over in my mind to make sure I had it right. (The year before in the UNLV semifinal game, I got so excited that I stumbled on the score a little bit which kept that call from being exceptionally good.) For some reason I never once thought about a three-pointer after the Duke timeout.

We came back from the break and reset the situation on the air. As the play started, out of the corner of my eye I saw Laettner coming to the top of the key. He caught the pass, turned, and hit an incredible shot. Laettner did so much in that 1.8 seconds, because I described it on the air as, "Laettner catches, comes down, dribbles (and there was a question mark in my voice as to why he was doing that), turns, shoots, scooooooores!"

To say the least, the scene became chaotic. The Duke players were in a state of  1983 was the first year in which the national champion had to win six games in the NCAA Tournament.

euphoria. Laettner was running around the court; Grant Hill was trying to chase Christian down to hug him. Then, for some reason, I looked down in front of me and saw Sean Woods lying prone on the floor, beating his head into the court. He could not believe the game was lost. Two minutes earlier he was the hero. It was unbelievable.

That was the last Wildcat game that legendary broadcaster Cawood Ledford called. After the game, Mike Krzyzewski went straight over to Cawood and asked to go on with him on the Kentucky network to talk to the Kentucky fans. That was something you don't see everyday.

After the 1992 regional finals with Kentucky, the Blue Devils went on to defeat Indiana, 81-78, and Michigan by 20 points for their second straight national title. That *was* a special team.

Laettner had a great game against Kentucky with 31 points, but he didn't have a very good Final Four. (In fact, he only had a total of 27 points in the two Final Four games.) Regardless, he became the first player in NCAA history to start in four Final Fours, and garnered the National Player of the Year award in the 1991-1992 season, his last as a Blue Devil.

Roy Williams

We had a great run in the 1991 NCAA Tournament, beating the Nos. 2, 3 and 4 teams in the country in our final three games to get to the championship against Duke. Each game, I told the guys that I thought they could do it, and as long as they believed they could, we would get it done.

We have had some good stretches where our team has played well against back-to-back tough opponents. However, none of my teams has ever had a stretch with the kind of magnitude that we had going up against Indiana in the regional semifinals, Arkansas in the regional finals, and Carolina in the national semifinals. I have never had a team play that well in games that big in, basically, a 10-day stretch. That was fantastic basketball for us, especially considering that the second half of the Arkansas game and the entire Indiana game weren't close.

Against Indiana, we jumped out to a 26-4 lead, and the Hoosiers never got closer than 12 points in the game. In the next game, against Arkansas, we were down by 12 at the half, and outscored the Razorbacks by 24 in the second half to win by 12. The third team in our run was North Carolina in the Final Four.

Before the game with the Tar Heels, all of the media questions were about me playing against Coach Dean Smith, not about Kansas facing North Carolina. That was a distraction, yet when we got to the arena, I completely forgot about Coach Smith and focused on us playing Carolina. The thought of Dean Smith sitting on the other bench never entered my mind, at least until the closing moments of the game.

I didn't like, or appreciate, the way the Carolina game ended with Coach Smith being ejected. He didn't deserve to have the technical to get ejected. I knew, as soon as it happened, that it would take away from the great victory of our team, and the media would want to talk about that instead of giving our kids credit. When Coach came by our bench on his way out of the arena he told me, "You know I did not plan this." I told him I knew.

He made the statement later that it was going to take away from a great Kansas victory and that he hated that. It really did take away from the kids, which bothered me. We were fortunate to win that one, 79-73, to reach the championship game against either Duke or UNLV.

Watching a little of that second semifinal game, I was mad at our fans because they were pulling for Duke to beat UNLV. Vegas was ranked No. 1 in the nation, but I felt we could fare better against the Runnin' Rebels because we had done so well during the previous three games in the huge underdog role. They were going to be such a huge favorite against us, that I thought our chances would be better against them than against Duke. Also, I knew our offensive philosophy would make it where we could play with Vegas better than people thought we would.

It was really nerve-racking trying to get out of the arena after the Carolina game to celebrate the fact that we were in a Final Four, because of all of the media requests. First we were delayed with CNN, then at ESPN I had to wait for an overtime hockey game that seemed like it was never going to end. After all of that and watching the Duke-UNLV game, I didn't get back to the hotel until midnight. All of the Kansas people had already celebrated and I was just getting back from the arena. So, instead of celebrating, I started looking ahead to the Blue Devils. For a little less than 48 hours it was total concentration, trying to think about what we could do to bother Duke on Monday night.

Our team got off to a bad start in the finals against the Blue Devils. On the first play of the night, we got the opening tap, but we threw the dad-gummed ball backcourt. Needless to say, that was not the way we wanted to start the championship game. Still, it was a pretty good basketball game for a while.

One of the most memorable

Final Four Fast Facts

Louisville is the only team to reach the Final Four in four different years during the 1980s.

Duke plays was a Bobby Hurley lob pass that looked like it was going out of bounds, when all of a sudden, Grant Hill caught the ball and dunked it. That blew my mind because I didn't think there was any way Hill was going to get to that ball.

At halftime I told the kids that we hadn't started playing yet. I felt that we hadn't really gotten into a rhythm. If we could have gotten a couple of shots to fall and get a couple defensive stops to get that rhythm into the game with some confidence, then I felt that we had a chance to win.

In the second half, we closed the game to within five points and had Duke trapped in the backcourt with eight seconds gone on the shot clock. The ninth second ticked away. The Duke player called a timeout before the backcourt violation. If we had gotten the turnover at that point, we may have been able to cut the score down to two or three points. The timeout was a smart play. They got the ball inbounds the next time, and scored that trip down the court.

Duke did a great job with dribble penetration and bothering us inside with Christian Laettner. We were off-balance the whole game. Alonzo Jamison led our team in field-goal percentage during the season, yet against Duke he was 1-for-10, with most of his shots coming three or four feet out. He never got it going. Duke's size bothered us. They were very athletic and deserve all of the credit for keeping us off-balance. Throughout the entire game, it felt like we were trying to come from behind every second. We never really got into the game to the point where we were doing anything other than treading water. We never could tie the score. Duke won the national championship with a 72-65 victory. Losing to the Blue Devils in the title game is the main thing that sticks out to me from the 1991 season, but they earned the championship.

CHAPTER 19

Minneapolis, Minnesota
April 4 & 6, 1992

Duke head coach Mike Krzyzewski enjoyed the feeling of winning his first NCAA national championship in 1991 so much, that he wanted to experience it again. Whereas most programs that win the tournament look forward to defending their title, that was a very real possibility for the Blue Devils. Duke only lost one player off its national title team, reserve forward Greg Koubek.

The main players from Duke's 1991 team consisted of one freshman, three sophomores and two juniors. All of those players, with another year of experience, were back for a repeat run, except Billy McCaffrey, who transferred to another school.

The biggest tournament scare for the Blue Devils came in the East Regional final against Kentucky in one of the most exciting NCAA games in the tournament's history. Following a timeout with less than two seconds left in overtime, and Kentucky leading 103-102, Grant Hill made a perfect baseball throw to Christian Laettner toward the top of the key, who spun and hit

Final Four Fast Facts

CBS Sports won an Emmy Award for its coverage of the 1982 North Carolina-Georgetown championship game.

the winning jumper to send the Blue Devils to the Final Four.

By the time the season was complete, Mike Krzyzewski and his Duke Blue Devils had done two things which are near-impossible in today's college game ... went wire to wire ranked No. 1 in the nation; and, repeated as national champions.

1992 All-Tournament Team

Grant Hill, Duke
Bobby Hurley, Duke
  (Most Outstanding Player)
Christian Laettner, Duke
Jalen Rose, Michigan
Chris Webber, Michigan

Final Four Participants

Cincinnati
Duke
Indiana
Michigan

National Semifinals

Michigan 76, Cincinnati 72
Duke 81, Indiana 78

National Championship

Duke 71, Michigan 51

Mike Krzyzewski

One of the things that I'm most proud of from my coaching career is how our 1991-1992 Duke team was ranked No. 1 in the nation, wire-to-wire. As hard as it is to win the national championship, not many teams have gone through the entire season ranked No. 1, while at the same time, repeating as national champions from the year before. It was incredible for me.

That season began for our team as soon as we returned to Durham after winning the first national championship in 1991, in terms of the psychological aspect and getting ourselves prepared. That was a very gratifying year, very fulfilling, but it was a long season because it began in April instead of October. For that reason, when we did win again in 1992, the sense of accomplishment was immense.

Winning a national championship is difficult whether it's a first, second or third title. Each year's final game is a singular event that really can't be compared to another national championship game. Each journey that you have, even to get to that game, is different. There are so many different factors from year to year such as the different team we have on the court and various injury problems throughout the season. It's a separate event each time and I try not to compare them at all.

When you try to compare the titles, each one is drastically different. For instance, we had to beat a very good UNLV team in the 1991 semifinals. UNLV had defeated us badly in the finals the previous year. After winning the 1991 title, and going through the next season in the No. 1 spot, people expected us to repeat. As far as our players and coaches were concerned, in the previous April, we felt that the 1992 title was meant to be for us. That's why it was such a long year. We just felt that it was our title to win, and if we did not attack and go after it the right way, we wouldn't get it. That team did what it needed to do throughout the whole year.

The 1992 team was injured a lot. People often don't remember, as we were going through January, we were kind of beating everybody big, but then Bobby Hurley broke his foot and was out for three-and-a-half weeks. As soon as he came back to the team, Grant Hill got hurt and was out for two weeks. So, for about a month, the team did not function together. Then, all of a sudden, shortly before the Atlantic Coast Conference Tournament, we came back together again. I still don't feel the team ever regained the form that it had in January. But, it made no excuses ... it just kept playing.

We had a great group of competitors, which is why, I think, we won. They had fun playing the game and playing together. Our style of basketball was not a restricted style. We attacked offensively and defensively with Hurley, who was the most daring player I have ever coached. When he led the fast break, he could make points for us. It was tough being conservative with Bobby Hurley on the team, because he attacked so well. To compliment Hurley's pressure on the fast break, we had great finishers in Grant Hill, Brian Davis, Thomas Hill and Antonio Lang. On top of all of that was Christian Laettner, who was the National Player of the Year that season.

The goal of that group was to repeat as national champions. Our closest call during the tournament came in a hard-fought East Regional Final game against Kentucky, in what many consider to be the greatest NCAA Tournament game of all time. With two seconds left in overtime, Kentucky's Sean Woods hit a bank shot to give the Wildcats a 103-102 lead. Having to go the length of the court to score in less than two seconds, we called a timeout.

There was an incredible letdown when Woods hit that shot. At that point during a timeout, the mood in the huddle has to be created by the coach, or by the players. I started to create the mood. I really felt we were going to win. I hate to use the word "destined," but we had gone too far to lose on a bank shot. Not that Kentucky didn't play great, because they did, but that particular shot kind of made me angry. Regardless, I still felt like we were going to win. The trick was going to be relating that to the players.

After about a minute, I could sense that our players felt that same way. I told them in the huddle that we were going to win. Once I saw in their eyes that they believed it, we mapped out some strategy.

Players make the plays happen; coaches don't. We had two exceptional players make that final play, with Grant Hill making the pass and Laettner making the catch, and having the poise to collect himself and hit the shot. You don't win without really good players. We got all of those players on the same track in the huddle during that last timeout, and it turned out great for us, as we earned a trip to the Final Four with a 104-103 win.

The semifinal game with Indiana was extremely difficult for us. The emotional expense that was created with Kentucky, especially for Laettner, was very evident in the Final Four. All of the awards that he had won, and the whole game with Kentucky, took a lot out of him.

We were lucky to be as close as we were with Indiana at halftime, trailing 42-37. Hurley had five 3-pointers in the first half. He let us down in the Seton Hall game during the Sweet 16, but in the first half of the Indiana game, he carried us on his back and kept us within striking distance of a really good Indiana team.

Whereas the Hoosiers outplayed us in the first half, we outplayed them in the second half, and came back to win, 81-78. It was a huge win, especially considering how thoroughly they outplayed us before halftime.

The only team standing between us and our goal now was Michigan. After another tight first half, we trailed 31-30 at the break. Our locker room was calm during halftime, except with the players. The 1992 Duke team had a special chemistry where the players spoke to each other bluntly. Some people, if they heard the guys talk to each other, might say that they didn't get along sometimes. Just the opposite was true. These guys got along so well that they could tell each other the truth, cut to the chase, and not worry about all that other baloney. During that halftime, they did. Their play in the second half was based more on what the players said than what I said.

Hurley, who usually let his play do the talking for him, even spoke up during that Michigan halftime. He offered what he felt would be needed for the team to step up and win in the second half. Certainly the play of all of those guys backed up what they said.

As with the Indiana game, we wore Michigan down in the second half. Our experience showed, especially that of Laettner. He had his worst half as a player at Duke in the first half of the championship game. I told him at halftime, and have joked with him since, that he threw the ball to Michigan more than he threw it to Duke in that first half.

After the intermission, however, Laettner showed the heart and mind of a champion, by really picking us up and coming up with a couple of key buckets. We started a string where we scored on 12-out-of-13 possessions, and basically broke the game open. It was Laettner during that time who hit a couple of key baskets for us. He ended up leading all scorers in the game with 19 points.

Grant Hill was another spark for us during that second half run, as he took over the baseline. Michigan could not stop him along the baseline, and he helped break the game open. He finished the night with 18 points.

Grant, to me, in both of those national championship years, could have been the Most Valuable Player of the Final Four. In 1991, his defense against UNLV and Kansas was sensational. He basically held their top scorers without any points. In the 1992 Final Four, he was the player that the other teams didn't have. Michigan and Indiana had  In 1982, CBS Sports televised the *Selection Show* live for the first time. great players, like Chris Webber and Calbert Cheaney, but Grant was remarkable. If the Final Four were a chess game, he would have been the queen, because he could move anywhere. As a result, he did.

That 1992 Duke team had the toughest road to travel than any of our other teams. That group was more mentally tough than any team I've coached. I don't even think they felt any pressure to perform, even though the only way they could be successful in the eyes of the public was to win it all. They did win it all and they had fun doing it. That shows how good they were. If Bobby and Grant hadn't gotten hurt in February, that team could have finished stronger. Regardless, they liked challenges, even when those guys were injured. We went down to Louisiana State without Bobby and beat Shaquille O'Neal and the Tigers with Grant as the point guard. Then, we went out to UCLA and won without Grant. The players seemed to like those sorts of challenges. I think it's one of the great teams of all time.

Their mental toughness and competitiveness was amazing, especially to be able to endure the challenges associated with being ranked No. 1 for the entire season, go to the Final Four and repeat as national champions. Going to the Final Four is an amazing event. The first time you go, in coaching and as a player, is like going to the Promised Land. People judge us by whether or not we went to the Promised Land ... they typically don't even judge a coach or player by winning a national championship.

Before reaching that first one you sometimes think, "I'm never going to get there." Then, all of a sudden, you're there with a chance to win a national championship! That feeling cannot be duplicated.

One of the reasons I try to live through my players during a Final Four is because I've been there. Now, I want to experience how they feel because it's usually the first time that they have gone. For me, the first time was the most thrilling. Certainly winning the title in 1991 and 1992 was amazing, but to get there for the first time was kind of a dream come true.

I will never forget that experience of going to the Final Four because it is a shared experience. When you share that experience with the type of kids and coaches that I've had an opportunity to work with, you can live it over and over again. For a tennis player, winning Wimbledon would be tough to share with anybody (although, believe me, I'd like to be a tennis player and win Wimbledon) because one person is winning it, instead of a team.

That's what coaching is about ... you get a chance to share these experiences with a really good group of players that you've recruited, put together, nurtured and have seen grow. To reach the Promised Land, and help those kids get there while, at the same time, they help you get there, is an incredible experience.

Final Four Fast Facts

Dean Smith is one of only two people (Bob Knight) to play (Kansas, 1952) and coach (North Carolina, 1982 and 1993) on a national championship team.

CHAPTER 20

New Orleans, Louisiana
April 3 & 5, 1993

T he Michigan Wolverines and the North Carolina Tar Heels each felt that the 1993 championship belonged to them. The Wolverines had been in the championship game in 1992 where they lost to Duke. They had been there. Playing in the last game of the year was still fresh in their minds throughout the 1992-1993 season, even when they defeated Carolina in the Rainbow Classic.

The Tar Heels felt a need to redeem themselves after the 1992 season, one in which they had lost nine games and were eliminated in the regional semifinals of the national tournament ... not a good season by Carolina standards. It became the team's mission in 1993, especially for the seniors, to prove that the 1992 campaign was a fluke.

Pat Sullivan is the type of player that any basketball coach would love to have on his team; a hard-worker with skills and smarts who is fundamentally sound. Even though he wasn't a starter, as a junior he played in all 38 games for the Tar Heels in 1992-1993. There were a couple of games during his career when he was brought off the bench for defensive purposes, but one of his strengths was in his free throw shooting. He finished his career at Carolina ranked 19th on the Tar Heels' all-time Free-Throw Shooting list (3rd over the past decade) at 77.4 percent. His free-throw shooting was a key against the Wolverines in the 1993 title game. With 20 seconds remaining in the game, Sullivan went to the line and hit the front-end of a one-and-one to give Carolina a two-point lead.

Sullivan has remained at Carolina as an assistant coach, first under Dean Smith and now with Bill Guthridge.

Pat Sullivan

T eamwork is vital to the success of a basketball team. The North Carolina Tar Heels have always been a program that thrives around that teamwork. During my first year at Carolina, 1990-1991, we made it to the Final Four against Kansas. That was a tight group with seniors King Rice, Rick Fox

1993 All-Tournament Team

George Lynch, North Carolina
Jamal Mashburn, Kentucky
Eric Montross, North Carolina
Chris Webber, Michigan
Donald Williams, North Carolina
  (Most Outstanding Player)

Final Four Participants

Kansas
Kentucky
Michigan
North Carolina

National Semifinals

Michigan 81, Kentucky 78 (OT)
North Carolina 78, Kansas 68

National Championship

UNC 77, Michigan 71

and Pete Chilcutt, and junior Hubert Davis. We were very close that year, and as freshmen we figured that we were at Carolina and this was how tight the team was supposed to be each year.

The next year, 1992, we were still close, but it wasn't quite like it had been in 1991. But, we weren't as good of a team, we didn't win as many ballgames, and we didn't make it to the Final Four ... that bothered us. We went to the Sweet 16 and lost to Ohio State, finishing that season with a record of 23-10. We slipped throughout that season by Carolina standards. We didn't feel

Final Four Fast Facts

The Kansas Jayhawks became the first unranked team and the first team with 10 or more losses (11) to win the national championship(1988).

good about ourselves after that season. After that loss to Ohio State, the 1993 senior class of Scott Cherry, George Lynch, Henrik Rodl, Travis Stephenson and Matt Wenstrom really dedicated their lives to wanting to have a great next season. As underclassmen, we saw that happening, and wanted to do particularly well.

The seniors didn't want to go out on a bad note, so they took it upon themselves to lead the team. They did a wonderful job. All five of the teams of which I was a part at North Carolina were extremely close, but the 1993 team, because of what happened the year before, decided that we were going to work better together.

That whole summer before the 1992-1993 season, our team did everything together from going to movies, to eating, to playing on the same softball teams. We were really a tight-knit group that got along great together. That unity carried on into the basketball season.

We met Michigan in December in the semifinals of the Rainbow Classic, and they beat us, 79-78, on a shot at the buzzer by Jalen Rose. That game, more than any game that season, gave us a lot of confidence to know that we could compete at the top level nationally. Michigan had been to the championship game the previous season, and before we played them in December, we didn't know if we could compete with them or not.

After losing to Michigan in the Rainbow Classic, we didn't lose again until back-to-back conference setbacks on the road at Wake Forest and at Duke. Those were our only two losses in the Atlantic Coast Conference, as we finished 14-2 in the league and were the regular-season ACC champs. Our only other loss of that season was in the ACC Tournament finals against Georgia Tech.

We then had a really, really good run in the NCAA Tournament, all the way to the championship game against Michigan.

Even though we lost to the Wolverines three months earlier, Coach Dean Smith never talked to us in terms of revenge. Instead, he always talked about going out and playing hard, playing smart and playing together. As a team we were driven at getting back at the Wolverines, and winning the title. George Lynch was always talking about winning the championship for Coach Smith. Lynch was really a catalyst on that team and was instrumental in all of us wanting to win it for Coach because, by his talking about it, made the idea carry over to everybody else on the team.

Playing for Coach Smith was incredible. I'm really honored to say that I had the opportunity to play for him. He taught us so much about basketball and how that can carry into our everyday lives in terms of discipline, teamwork, being unselfish, saying thank you, being on time, among other things that are so important in everyday life. He taught us those things on and off the court. Coach was like a father figure to all of the guys.

He definitely had an influence in my wanting to pursue coaching. Seeing him diagram a play is almost like watching a choreographer with a dance. He was so good at not only drawing up the play, but then telling us what the other team was going to do.

I'll never forget the 1993 regional finals where we went into overtime with Cincinnati. There were eight seconds left in the game and, with the ball under our basket, Coach Smith called a timeout and drew up a play. He said, "Brian (Reese) you run to the corner. Eric (Montross), you screen them. They'll switch, so Brian, come off and you'll be wide open. Then Derrick, just throw the ball up to Brian. Brian, you won't have time to dunk it, so just jump up and drop it in the basket and we'll win." I knew Coach Smith was a great coach, but I had my doubts as to whether or not this would work.

Sure enough, the play worked out exactly as Coach said, including the Cincinnati players making the defensive switch. The only problem was that Brian tried to dunk the ball and he clanked it off the rim and missed it. But, seeing that play executed the way Coach said it would be was the most incredible thing. The game went into overtime. We were all shell-shocked. If you ever see a video of that, look at our faces ... it looks like we had lost that game even though it was going into overtime. Coach was just clapping and smiling, saying that we would get it in over-time. Sure enough, we did, winning 75-68 and earning a trip to the Final Four.

Knowing that Coach Smith was on our side, especially in a tight game, we knew we were not going to lose. Coach was so calm and poised on the sidelines that we couldn't help but have that positive atti-tude. That demeanor carried over into the way we played on the court. Whether we were down by one point or 10 points, we knew we could come back and win.

In a regular-season game at home against Florida State, we were down by 21 points with nine minutes to play, but Coach was calm as could be. We hit a three-pointer to cut the Seminole lead to 18, and Coach called a timeout. He told us to just relax and see what happens. We came back and won the game, 82-77.

So, even though the championship game with Michigan was nip and tuck the whole way, we knew winning was a definite possibility. Since

Final Four Fast Facts

Memphis State was the only non-Big East school in the 1985 Final Four.

we had played the Wolverines in December, we had a tremendous amount of confidence that we could win. It certainly helped that they had beaten us in that earlier game. Not to say they weren't hungry for a national championship, because they obviously were, but we felt that we owed them one.

We were up by one point with 20 seconds left in the game when I had the ball in my hands, wondering if I should pass it or hold on to it and get fouled. Considering I was more nervous about throwing the ball away than going to the line, I got fouled and was headed to the stripe for a one-and-one. Before shooting, I looked over at our bench and saw all of my teammates. The thoughts of the summer before that season, and all of the time that we spent together having fun and working hard, ran through my mind. I didn't want to let any of those guys down because I knew how much the championship meant to all of them.

I was more worried about letting the other Tar Heels down than I was about actually missing the free throws. The Michigan players weren't going to let me go to the line in quiet, either. Jalen Rose, Juwan Howard and Chris Webber were egging me on, telling me how the free throws were for the championship, and that type of thing. As it turned out, I hit the first shot and missed the second one.

Less than 10 seconds later, our championship was sealed when, with 11 seconds remaining, Michigan's Chris Webber called a timeout that the Wolverines didn't have. Donald Williams hit the free throws for us. For the most part, as a player I think it's easy to empathize with Webber in that situation. I can't speak for how Michigan handled those types of situations, but for the Tar Heels, we were not allowed to call timeouts unless Coach Smith was calling for one. At Carolina, timeouts are like gold.

I could definitely see where a kid might dribble down the court and, not feeling comfortable with the situation, call a timeout. And who knows, there may have been guys on the sidelines yelling for Webber to call a timeout, so he did. I've seen a video of a guy on the Michigan bench signaling for a timeout after Michigan got the rebound.

If someone ever tried to tarnish or take away from Carolina's great win, and Coach Smith's great win, because of Webber's timeout, then I would definitely think that too much of a big deal has been made about it. With 11 seconds left, Michigan would still have had to come down the court and made a shot for the tie, or a 3-pointer for the lead. Hopefully the timeout is not what people think cost Michigan the game. It obviously helped us win, but it didn't determine the outcome of the game.

We prided ourselves on our team defense, and a lot of that pressure on Webber to call the timeout has to be credited to the defensive play of Derrick Phelps and George Lynch, who trapped Chris in the backcourt. Derrick, as the point guard, loved playing defense and taking the other team's point guard out of the game. He really made it easier on all of us to apply pressure on people and deny passes because we never had to worry about Phelps getting beat. He loved the challenge of playing against bigger point guards.

Phelps ended the game with only nine points, but he hit a couple big shots for us. He was great. He had hurt his back about two or three weeks before the championship, and was playing through the whole tournament with a great deal of pain.

Lynch was the warrior on our team. There were times in that game and throughout that tournament when Lynch refused to let the team lose because he wanted to win so badly for Coach Smith. He didn't necessarily care about winning for George Lynch, he wanted it for Dean Smith. Looking back, that was a special thing. Lynch really helped our whole mindset that weekend, making it a business first attitude. He figured we would have fun after we won the tournament. (Although, as we found out, his idea of having fun after winning in New Orleans was to go back to his hotel room, order a pizza and watch sports on television. That was the big, exciting weekend for George Lynch.)

Going to the Final Four was both special and unforgettable. The thing that makes it even more special for me is the fact that I'm one of only eight Carolina players to play on three Final Four teams. Before me, the only other Tar Heels to do that were from the 1967-1968-1969 teams. At the time when we won the title in 1993, we were all 18-22 year old kids, and didn't really think about the experience of winning. We had a great time winning, and relished it for the next couple of days, but then we kind of forgot about it. Now, seven years later, it's something I appreciate a lot more. Every year the memory gets better and better because it becomes more amazing that only one team is going to win each year. Watching Connecticut win the championship in 1999 almost brought tears to my eyes thinking that we did that once.

Words really can't express that emotion,

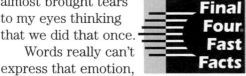

In 1989, Steve Fisher (Michigan) became the first head coach to win the national championship in his first year.

or that feeling, of the moment when the final buzzer goes off and you realize you have won the national championship. The feeling is something that only the teams that have won the tournament can describe. Those kids on the 1999 UConn team probably felt the same way we felt back in 1993, which is probably the same way the Tar Heels felt in 1982 when they won it. I couldn't even tell any of the guys that I coach now what winning it really felt like, unless they have experienced it. Hopefully they'll get that opportunity soon.

CHAPTER 21

St. Petersburg, Florida
March 27 & 29, 1999

There is an "old" game that (particularly) boys like to play called King of the Hill. The object is to knock everyone off the dirt pile (or have someone do that for you) and be the last one standing at the top. The 1998-1999 National College Basketball Poll was much the same way, with only two teams willing to share the top spot ... Connecticut and Duke.

Oddly, the Huskies and Blue Devils met each other in the 1999 NCAA Tournament championship game. Even though the Huskies had been the only other top-ranked team in 1998-1999, they weren't given much of a chance to beat Duke. Actually, no team was given any chance to beat the "unbeatable" Duke Blue Devils.

After reaching the 1998 Elite Eight, UConn set all of its 1999 goals toward St. Petersburg. Why should 1999 be any different for the program that had never reached the Final Four? Head coach Jim Calhoun, who has been at the Husky helm for 14 years, said he felt that it was a special season for UConn. On a bizarre note ... including the title game, the Huskies trailed at halftime in 10 games during 1998-1999. They won each of those 10 games.

The Duke Blue Devils were the team that most people had assumed would win the title. They were an impressive, loaded team that had been simply dominating through the second half of the year. The team was young and talented enough that two titles weren't completely out of the question. Heading into the championship game with Connecticut, Duke had won 32 straight games.

Although it was hardly the same magnitude of Villanova beating Georgetown in 1985, as some sportswriters have suggested, the Huskies beating the Blue Devils could be considered an upset. Maybe even a big upset.

Gregg Doyel covers primarily the Duke Blue Devils for *The Charlotte Observer*. He is the author of *Coach K: Building the Duke Dynasty*. Calhoun, after leading his team to the 1999 title, now has the daunting challenge of defending UConn's spot on the dirt hill.

1999 All-Tournament Team

Elton Brand, Duke
Khalid El-Amin, Connecticut
Richard Hamilton, Connecticut
  (Most Outstanding Player)
Trajan Langdon, Duke
Ricky Moore, Connecticut

Final Four Participants

Connecticut
Duke
Michigan State
Ohio State

National Semifinals

Connecticut 64, Ohio State 58
Duke 68, Michigan State 62

National Championship

Connecticut 77, Duke 74

Jim Calhoun

Our UConn team had come off a pretty good season in 1998 when we reached the Elite Eight, but after losing to North Carolina in that regional championship, we made it our goal to reach the 1999 Final Four. We had never been to the Final Four, although we had been to the regional finals. The 1998-1999 team was going to be a talented enough group to make it a special season.

In order to look at the NCAA Tournament run, I think it's important to see how things went during the regular season. Because of an unexplained loss and a couple key injuries in the regular season, the maturity our team showed through the tournament was largely developed in the season.

After a couple of early wins, including one over Michigan State, we started to struggle, even though we were winning some games. As we hit the holiday break, we were just okay. We were still winning, with a record of 8-0, but we weren't beating some of these teams as easily as we should have been.

One thing that turned out to be good for us was the NBA player's strike. Ray Allen, Travis Knight, Scott Burrell and Donyell Marshall, all former UConn players who are in the NBA, started hanging around campus because they wanted to get back into shape in case the rumors of the strike ending were true. We were able to utilize those guys over a practice period of two weeks. All of a sudden our practices, which had been good, started to take on a different light. It was terrific for us from the standpoint of great competition but also our guys could see the work ethic of these NBA players.

The first game after those practices was against a solid Villanova team. We won 100-76. Our players really turned it up a notch. For the next 10 games or so, we were awfully good. I felt we were as good at that point as anybody in the country.

On January 30, still ranked No. 1, we played St. John's at Madison Square Garden in New York. It was an absolute war with them, but we escaped with a four-point win, 78-74. Both teams played a fabulous game. We felt good about ourselves with the win, and appeared to be over the hump. At least that was the thought.

The next morning, Sunday, as we were getting ready to start practice to prepare for a nationally televised game with Syracuse on Monday, Richard (Rip) Hamilton was going to have an MRI done on his thigh and Jake Voskuhl's foot was sore (although at the time we didn't think much about that). On Monday, x-rays showed that Jake had a stress fracture in his left foot, and Rip's MRI showed a hematoma in his thigh.

We played Syracuse that night without Jake and Rip and lost, 42-59. I list our 42 first because that score is so bad. No team of mine at UConn in 14 years had scored only 42 points. It was the fewest number of points that any UConn team had scored in 27 years. To make that score seem worse, we hit a 3-pointer with about 10 seconds left to bring the score up to 42. We were awful that night. It was hard to believe that we had just put together a 19-game win streak.

Four days later, we were in California to play No. 4 Stanford. We beat them 70-59 in front of an electric crowd, in a great basketball game. That night I sat there with myself and thought that maybe our team had something special. We had just bounced back from a horrible performance to improve to 20-1 with a win over a tough Stanford team.

The season had two or three different aspects to it with the great stretch run from December 23 all the way to the St. John's game where we were fabulous. Then we had to work over the last month of the season to get healthy and whole, mentally and physically.

With a win over the tournament surprise, Gonzaga, we earned our first-ever trip to the Final Four. After a hard-fought semifinal win over Ohio State, we were set to play Duke for the title on Monday night. There is no question that the attention Duke received throughout the tournament made our guys want the title even more. I even tried to help as much as possible by saying how good Duke was, even though I never believed they were better than us. They did have more offensive talent than us, but any of Duke's opponents could have said that.

If that Blue Devil team had come back intact for the 1999-2000 season, the NCAA might have had to declare them illegal ... Duke could have been that good. Corey Maggette was a freshman in 1999 who could score points, but he was a freshman defensively. William Avery was starting to come into his own as the point guard. Elton Brand was probably as good as any player in college basketball. The Blue Devils were incredibly talented, but they didn't have the grit, maturity, or, quite frankly, the experience of being behind in ballgames.

Going into that game, we had trailed at halftime nine times during the season. Duke led at halftime of the championship game. So, our team trailed at halftime 10 times, winning all 10 games. We felt that if you were leading at the half, we had you right where we wanted you. It's a bizarre statistic, but I'm not sure that anyone else during the season has trailed at halftime that many times then won the title.

We had something very special as a team with great leadership from guys like Hamilton, Voskuhl, Kevin Freeman and Ricky Moore. Mentally  we were a very tough team from various things that happened over the previous two or three years.

In 1987, Indiana became the first program to win the NCAA title in four different decades.

The fact that people, and rightly so, gave Duke so much praise during the tournament was to our advantage. The Blue Devils did dominate the last half of the basketball season, so it wasn't undeserving praise. The funny thing to me is that virtually no one compared scores of teams that both Duke and UConn had played. For instance, Duke played St. John's in an overtime game. Three weeks later, we played St. John's, led at halftime by 19 points, had leads in the 30s, and won by 20. Michigan State was another common opponent. Enough comparisons could have been done to realize that it was going to be a heck of a national championship game.

Duke jumped ahead of us, 9-2, to start the game, but we countered with a 15-4 run to take the lead. There were so many critical parts to the game for us, but that was definitely a main one. I did not want to get into a wild shootout with the Blue Devils, nor did I want them to feel that they could dominate us. During a couple timeouts when we were behind, I kept stressing to the kids that we were fine. That 15-4 run was important to tell Duke, "Hold on, you're not going anywhere."

Coming down the stretch, we hit a 3-pointer to take the lead. A couple minutes later, with less than a minute to play, William Avery hit his free throws in a one-and-one situation to bring the Blue Devils back to within one point. We had to make one more big play, and Khalid El-Amin did. With about five seconds left, he hit two free throws to give us a three-point lead. Langdon lost the ball out of bounds right before the buzzer, and we had the national championship, 77-74.

I could explain the feeling I had as the final few seconds ticked off in the Gonzaga game, which put us in the Final Four, but I truly don't remember the last seconds of the Duke game because I was still so involved in worrying about the foul situation and whether or not our guys were going to play tight enough defense. When the horn went off, I walked over to say something to Michael [Krzyzewski], who was terrific as usual. Still, I was thinking about this as more of a game that we had just won. My mind still was racing. I've seen the tape a couple of times, and I had this blank stare on my face because I was still coaching. A few minutes later, as people were running around like crazy, I thought that's great, they're excited because we just won a game. Then it hit me, we had just won the national championship.

It was one of those things that as soon as the final horn went off in the Ohio State semifinal game, my attention turned to how we were going to beat this terrific Duke basketball team (yet I had watched them enough times that I knew we could beat them).

In 1983, Jimmy Valvano ran around the court looking for someone to hug. I was looking for a reason to hug somebody because to me we had just won a game, not the national championship. I had been so engrossed in the game that I just didn't get a chance until two or three minutes after the game to truly appreciate what our kids had just done.

I have run nine marathons. All my friends used to come and they had a party beforehand. Then during the marathon it's a big celebration for them, anticipating the finish. Over three hours later, you come off the course, dead tired, they throw a blanket on you, put you in the back of the car and everybody goes out for a spaghetti dinner. As a coach at the Final Four, it's analogous to a certain degree because everybody around you is having a great party except you. I enjoyed the atmosphere, and I made sure the kids enjoyed it. Clearly, when we got there, we were there to work. We just treated the Final Four like two road games where we were going to have some fun surrounded by a lot of pomp and circumstance. We got down to Florida on Wednesday and had fun with the kids. By late Thursday afternoon we were into our game mode.

Our fans had a great time. I'm sure that if someone had tried to rob banks or stores in the state of Connecticut during the championship, they probably could have had free rein, because many of our fans were in Florida.

If, God willing, we're fortunate enough to go back to a Final Four again, it probably won't feel quite the same as 1999, the first one. For our whole state of 3.6 million people, the 1999 Final Four really was a mystical, magical tour.

Since we won, it's been great to share this experience with my former players, our UConn basketball family, and my own family. With the state of Connecticut, though, it's been an absolutely, incredible experience to see how much the state has wrapped its arms around the championship as their own, which I really think is cool.

We were regionally a terrific team but we were never a national player. This championship has allowed us to be a national player which has made it even better. What made the 1999 national championship even more special for us was the fact that it was against Mike Krzyzewski and Duke. They epitomize, to me, the best team in the 1990s in college basketball. We were very fortunate to beat a great team and a great coach.

Gregg Doyel

History was waiting on the 1999 Duke basketball team, pointing its long finger at the Blue Devils, beckoning them onward, inward, to join the select group of teams known as the best ever in college basketball.

"They have to finish the job," Kansas coach Roy Williams said before the 1999 national championship game. "But they're the best team I've seen in 21 years of being a college coach, and if they do finish the job, then you can argue they're one of the best teams of all time."

San Francisco with Bill Russell in 1955-56. UCLA with Lew Alcindor in the late 1960s and Bill Walton in the early '70s. N.C. State with David Thompson in 1974. Indiana with Quinn Buckner in 1976. Duke, with Elton Brand, in 1999.

History was waiting.

So was Connecticut.

The 1999 title game at Tropicana Field was supposed to be Duke's coronation, but the Huskies crashed the party, ambushing the Blue Devils 77-74 in a thriller that saw neither team lead by more than seven points and wasn't decided until Duke All-American Trajan Langdon, who had 25 points, lost control of the ball at the buzzer as he tried to find an open three-pointer.

"They played great and we played great, but they did it a little better at the end," Duke coach Mike Krzyzewski said. "It was that kind of game. It was a great game. I don't feel bad about that game, and anyone who thinks I do doesn't know me very well."

Dwarfed by the Duke monster, Connecticut had to be one of the most underappreciated national finalists in NCAA men's basketball history. The Huskies entered the game with a 33-2 record and as one of only two teams all season (along with Duke, of course) to be ranked No. 1 in the country. Despite all that, Connecticut was reduced in pregame hype to the Little Engine That Could - the lovable underdog hoping to reach the top of Duke Mountain.

The Blue Devils had been scary good, becoming the first team to blow through the Atlantic Coast Conference with a 16-0 mark, winning those games by an average of 25 points, and losing just once in its first 38 games. The loss came at 2 a.m., North Carolina time, in November against Cincinnati in Alaska, but it had happened so far away, so late at night, and so long ago, it seemed like more of a myth than fact. Duke lost? Yeah, right.

Duke was hot. Duke was happening. Actor Kevin Costner dropped by Tropicana Field for the championship game, and he sat in the Duke section.

The stands also featured most of the top coaches in the country, many of whom were buzzing about Duke. Bill Guthridge, coach of the rival North Carolina Tar Heels, said he had never seen, in more than 30 years of college coaching, one team that was so much better than the rest of the country. Temple's John Chaney, whose team lost in the East Regional final to Duke, called the Blue Devils one of the best teams he had ever seen. "Whoever plans to beat Duke," Chaney said, "had better believe in God."

Connecticut, apparently, believed.

UConn? U-Can.

"They hadn't been challenged in close games all year," Connecticut forward Kevin Freeman said afterward. "But we win close games. We wanted to prove we are the best team in the country and we did."

What happened was, Connecticut stood up to the Duke monster. And the monster began to crumble. It was little things. Duke players rarely bicker, but there in the first half was Langdon, the senior captain, scolding sophomore backcourt mate William Avery for not clearing out of the way as Langdon dribbled against the press. Hemmed in by two defenders – his, plus Avery's – Langdon rushed a pass to Chris Carrawell, who couldn't handle it and traveled.

Instead of setting up its offense with a 9-2 lead, Duke lost the ball to Connecticut, which scored 15 of the next 19 points.

Duke was in a fight, and if the Blue Devils weren't sure on this point, Connecticut's Edmund Saunders made it very clear with 10 minutes left in the half. Duke's superstar, 6-foot-8, 265-pound Elton Brand, rose for a shot and Saunders blocked it out of bounds with such authority that Brand was knocked to the floor. As Brand lay there, Saunders loomed over him and looked down at the National Player of the Year, much as Muhammad Ali had over the fallen Sonny Liston roughly 35 years earlier in a heavyweight title fight.

Brand already had endured a frustrating stretch that began when he stepped prematurely into the lane on a missed Connecticut free throw, giving the Huskies a second shot (it also missed). Brand then lost a defensive rebound and saw it go to Connecticut's Souleymane Wane, who scored. On Duke's next possession, the irked Brand was called for an offensive foul as he swung an elbow at Wane. Then, the block by Saunders.

"They made it really difficult, dropping down (to double-team), fighting every time I touched the ball," Brand said later.

Meanwhile, the Blue Devils' offense stagnated under the Huskies' swarming, double-team defensive strategy against Brand. Carrawell's defender, Connecticut All-American forward Richard Hamilton, routinely left to help cover Brand, but Carrawell took only seven shots, making three.

At one point in the first half, when Carrawell went to the bench, Krzyzewski stopped him and urged, "Take the shot, Chris."

Other than Brand (15 points, 13 rebounds) and Langdon, who was 5-for-10 on three-pointers, Duke's other three starters — Avery, Carrawell and Shane Battier - were a combined 8-for-26 from the floor for 26 points.

Near the end of the first half Duke began to make uncharacteristically sloppy mistakes. After Hamilton missed a three-pointer, Langdon and freshman Corey Maggette fought for the rebound. Both lost. The ball popped out of bounds.

Langdon told Maggette, "I had the ball."

Maggette answered, "Me, too. Me first."

Avery, Duke's point guard, was having his own problems with his former high school teammate in Augusta, Ga., Connecticut's Ricky Moore. Known for his defense, Moore had 13 points in the first half, most coming against Avery, who couldn't stop Moore's penetration into the lane for short jumpers. After one such Moore foray into the lane, which ended in an Avery foul, Moore hopped up and down, faced the Duke cheering section and shouted: "Can't guard me! Can't guard me!"

Duke couldn't hit layups, either. Carrawell missed a breakaway after stealing a pass, and on Duke's next possession Battier missed an equally open layup after catching a pass under the basket from the double-teamed Brand.

Through it all Krzyzewski was working the officials with a zeal he hadn't shown much during the season. His players took his cue. Langdon bickered with a referee over a non-call but had the discussion cut short by Krzyzewski, who told his captain to get back on defense.

The first half was sluggish, neither team making much of an offensive statement beyond the shooting of Connecticut's Hamilton and Duke's Langdon. The Blue Devils began clicking early in the second as Langdon capitalized on his earlier outside shooting by blowing past close-covering Huskies guard Khalid El-Amin, drawing defenders and opening passing lanes all over the court. Duke opened a 48-43 lead on dunks by Brand and Battier, set up by passes from Avery and Carrawell, and appeared to be another possession or two from pulling away.

Connecticut answered, going on a 14-5 run for a 57-53 lead. Hamilton, who finished with a game-high 27 points, hit a three-pointer with 10:28 to play, and the Huskies had their biggest lead at 62-57.

That's about where the margin stayed for the next nine

Larry Brown and Frank McGuire are the only two coaches to lead two schools to the NCAA championship game.

minutes - the Huskies leading by four or five points - and Duke trailed 73-69 with 95 seconds left.

After a Connecticut miss, Langdon buried a three-pointer. The Huskies' lead was cut to 73-72.

It was time for the pudgy kid from Minnesota to become a star.

El-Amin, Connecticut's sophomore point guard, is listed at 5-10, 200 pounds. Both numbers are generous. El-Amin is shorter and squattier, his doughy upper body making his jersey look like a garbage bag filled with newspaper.

Having El-Amin as your point guard, Connecticut coach Jim Calhoun said before the championship game, was like buckling into a roller-coaster. Not smooth. Not necessarily fun all the time. But not boring, not ever.

"The great thing is we always end up at the top," Calhoun said. "Like any emotional person, and I don't know anybody like him that is that emotional, I relate a lot to how he is, what he does."

El-Amin had no problem with the analogy.

"He meant that in a positive way. We're similar people in that we love to compete, love to win and that's what drives us," El-Amin said. "That's the biggest thing, and the most important thing that we have in common."

Now, El-Amin and Calhoun were about to have something else to share: a national championship, the first in Connecticut history. After Langdon's three-pointer made it 73-72, El-Amin drove the lane and sank a short jumper to make it 75-72 with 1:05 to play. Eleven seconds later, Avery was fouled and hit both free throws to cut the margin back to a point, 75-74.

After an El-Amin miss in lane traffic, Langdon took the season into his hands. He had scored 20 points in the previous 21 minutes, but now he was locked with Moore, the Connecticut defensive stopper. Langdon got into the lane, picked up his dribble, spun ... and traveled with 5.4 seconds left.

The inbounds pass went to El-Amin, who was fouled with 5.2 seconds left. After he sank the first free throw, El-Amin turned to Avery, standing behind the foul line, and gloated.

"My game!" El-Amin screamed at Avery above the crowd noise. "This is my game!"

Moore, standing next to Avery, looked over and laughed in his former high school teammate's face.

Amin made the second free throw, too, for a 77-74 lead.

Duke had a timeout to use, but didn't use it. Krzyzewski didn't want to give the Huskies a chance to set up their defense. He wanted Langdon to use his experience as a fifth-year senior to get the Blue Devils into overtime. Langdon dribbled frantically down the court, through traps, but lost the ball out of bounds trying to get through one tight spot too many. The horn sounded. Game over.

Afterward, responding to media questions that made Langdon the goat, Krzyzewski was incredulous.

"I want the ball in Trajan's hands, and if we had to do it over again, I'd do the same thing," Krzyzewski said. "I'll go anywhere with Trajan Langdon. He can take the last shot for me any time. He tried to make a play, and unfortunately Connecticut made a better play. That's basketball.

"I don't think our kids showed they were under pressure. They were beating us and we came back, and in the last eight minutes we played our best basketball. Connecticut is really good, and we just came up a little short."

In the end, the 37-2 Duke team made its mark on history, after all. The 1998-99 Blue Devils will go down as one of the best teams ever in college basketball — one of the best teams who didn't win it all, rather.

Houston in 1983.

UNLV in 1991.

Duke in 1999.

CHAPTER 22

Behind the Scenes - Terry Ewert, Eric Mann

Since acquiring the rights to the NCAA Division I Men's Basketball Championship in 1982, CBS Sports has turned three weeks in March into a national obsession. The Network's buzzer-to-buzzer coverage of the tournament and the nation's bracket-by-bracket interest is unparalleled. Viewers see a product that has developed over many years and evolved into near flawless sports television programming.

At CBS Sports, the year-round efforts of many are lead by executive producer, Terry Ewert and coordinating producer, Eric Mann. Ewert joined the Network in 1997 after 18 years in senior production positions at NBC and four years as head of broadcasting for the Atlanta Olympic Organizing Committee. Mann, joined CBS Sports in 1981, just one year before the Network tipped-off tournament coverage. He began his career as a broadcast associate and currently oversees production for CBS Sports' studio shows.

TERRY EWERT

My greatest and most disappointing tournament moments occurred simultaneously. It was one of the occasions in my position as executive producer, when my heart crossed paths with my head. It was an all-at-once thrilling professional victory and heart sinking loss. This moment did not occur during a Final Four. It was simply another first round game in the 1998 tournament.

But this was not just another game to me. It was the end of the second day in the tournament and little Valaparaiso was on its way to defeating the No. 4 seed, Ole Miss, my alma mater. As has become the custom at CBS Sports, we made a move to switch every audience in the nation from their game of regional interest to the unlikely conclusion of the Valaparaiso-Ole Miss game. Believe me, it is not as easy as it looks. The combination of good technical timing and good luck is everything in the switching business. Once you make the decision to move you hope for the best and really root for an exciting outcome that warrants the change.

Valaparaiso had fought a hard contest against the Rebels. The

177

Stories From the Final Four

Crusaders' Bryce Drew hit a shot from deep outside for the win. When the ball went in, the control room cheered. My head dropped. Professionally, CBS Sports provided pictures of the tournament as it should be. It was a storybook moment with the unlikely hero, Bryce, being coached by his father, Homer Drew.

Rob Evans, now the head coach at Arizona State, had coached the Rebels through a truly phenomenal season. Homer and Bryce Drew brought that season to an even more phenomenal ending.

As an alumnus, I enjoyed the amazing University of Mississippi season. The Rebels had made it to the tournament for only the third time in the school's history (1981 and 1997 were the only two appearances). 1998 was supposed to be the chance to win their first-ever game in the tournament. Unfortunately for the Rebels, it didn't happen that day. And I was part of the committee that made sure the whole nation was there to witness.

History has taught CBS Sports that during each tournament there will be two or three Cinderella teams. No one predicted Gonzaga's run to the regional championship in 1999.

There will always be another Valaparaiso, another Gonzaga, another unpredictable Cinderella for America to fall in love with.

While it is true that sports fans like to watch the super teams like Duke and Connecticut, college basketball fans across the nation have always been charmed by the Cinderella. It is our job to see the story of those teams unfold and to introduce those stories and their very special characters to the national television audience.

The 1999 championship game between UConn and Duke is among my most memorable games to date. In essence, the two teams that had jockeyed all season for the top spot in the polls had reached the championship. CBS had a fairy tale match-up. The only two teams that held the No. 1 position in the polls all season would make things very dramatic.

On one side was Jim Calhoun, who never brought home the trophy. On the other, was Mike Krzyzewski of Duke, who had won the title previously. The fact that Coach K and Duke had been the nemesis of UConn getting to the championship made a very good television story.

Over time, coaches have learned to put on a game face with the press. They don't show nerves. The Final Four gives us an opportunity to spend time with coaches in a one-on-one setting the day before the game. While they usually hold back a lot of true emotion with the media, the environment exposes coaches behind their guard. In 1999 we visited with Coach Calhoun in a lobby breakfast area where he gave us a half hour of his time. He was very emotional about the Huskies' trip to the

Final Four. He felt this trip was not only about his current team, but also all the players that had contributed to his program during the nine years prior. Over nearly a decade, each player had made a contribution to getting to this season, to getting to this team. He was not nervous. But he was emotional as he named many individual players by name. It was inspirational. It was the kind of thing that makes the Final Four something more that just a national championship. It was about tradition. It was about loyalty. It was about work and effort. It was about winning and losing.

From a production standpoint, I am particularly proud of that 1999 title game. CBS Sports remained true to the story of the journey for these two teams. The pictures told the story that was before us, a true battle for No. 1.

THE CBS CHAMPIONSHIP

We were thrilled to learn that CBS was awarded the tournament through the year 2013. We love our relationship with the NCAA. We deal with a good committee comprised of former coaches, former athletic directors, current athletic directors and commissioners of conferences. They all have a passion for the sport of college basketball. They are all in favor of pushing the envelope in the game of college basketball to make it better. It's a pleasure working with people who understand that. I'm not suggesting that there are not other leagues that do that, because I think all of them are trying to understand how important television is to certain things in their sport. I just think that the people at the NCAA have been very understanding when we've thrown new ideas at them. They're very receptive. It's a good committee. I worked on an Olympic committee before the 1996 games in Atlanta. That was, at times, a bad committee. The NCAA's is a good one.

AND THE WINNER IS ...

The emotion of the Final Four really starts with the Sunday selection show before the tournament begins. Part of our deal with the NCAA is that we would have exclusive rights to carry the selection show live. We used to announce all 64 teams in the first five minutes of the show. That didn't make sense to me. As a result, we started spreading the announcement out over the entire 30-minute show. They aren't going to announce the Academy Award winners at the top of the show. Our show is sort of an Academy Awards-type show because there are teams out there that are genuinely surprised to get in the tournament.

Our ratings soared because we changed the format that way. It adds to the drama of the show. Who of the bubble teams are going to make it into the draw? It makes it very exciting to wait and see which teams make it. The selection show, which we first aired live in 1982, always gets great ratings. All of network television has seen an erosion during the last several years, but there is still a great deal of interest in seeing who makes it into the tournament.

The emotion of the Final Four is brought out by the camera shots, concentrating on not only the field of play, but also the bench area. We've been doing the tournament enough years that we know from where that emotion is going to come. Sometimes we shoot family members in the stands. We are now allowed to spend some time in the locker room before and after a game.

The tightness of the shots on faces, and the emotion involved with those faces, helps us bring out that drama. The great thing about a host city like Indianapolis is that the place is so basketball crazy, the fans help make our broadcasts better. We beg for the crowd to get into the game and understand it.

Eric Mann

The list of memorable teams, games and moments from the Final Four is seemingly endless. Michael Jordan hitting "the shot" as a freshman for North Carolina against Georgetown in 1982. The 1985 Villanova Wildcats beating Georgetown ... the giants being slain. Michigan's Chris Webber calling the timeout that the Wolverines didn't have in 1993. Tyus Edney leading UCLA to the title in 1995, including his coast-to-coast drive to beat Missouri in the second round.

One of the most vivid Final Fours that comes to mind for me is the 1983 title game with head coach Jim Valvano and North Carolina State at the Pit in New Mexico. That was a magical night. Throughout the tournament, the Wolfpack had some unbelievable wins.

As N.C. State advanced in the tournament, everybody remained skeptical. The team kept winning, and the story kept growing. People started to wonder who was this Valvano guy (at that time he wasn't very well known). For us, getting underdog stories like that is great.

In 1998 CBS Sports had the Valparaiso story with the father-son, coach-player, Homer and Bryce Drew. The team wasn't known, but it kept winning and people had to start taking note. We always want the big teams to advance because people are drawn to the teams like Duke, Kentucky and Kansas, but there is always room for the underdog. That's why the Valpo story was so great. Everywhere we went, people were talking about Bryce and Homer Drew.

A CBS crew went to the Drews' house and saw the basket where they practiced while Bryce was growing up. We did a nice piece at his house in the backyard. It's a great story. You can't beat that stuff.

The unknown people that you meet along the road to the Final Four are great for us. Introducing the viewer to new people is something we like to do a lot. As these teams advance in the tournament, it gives us, as the public, even more time to realize there are some amazing stories, and great tales, out there.

We sit in the studio in amazement at some of those great events.

A "TYPICAL" DAY...

Once March begins, the production schedule becomes close to 24 hours a day. There is usually a ton of coverage during *Selection Show Sunday* with games and shows building up to the NCAA announcing the teams that made the tournament.

When first-round games start on Thursday, the production team gets to the studio around 7 a.m. and, for the most part, with the exception of a couple hours of sleep, leave on Sunday night between 7:30 and 8:00 p.m. Since we're on the air the next day, we usually critique our work after each day. When CBS Sports goes off the air at 1:00 a.m., we'll still be there planning for the next day and seeing what worked in that day's coverage and what didn't. We're constantly fine-tuning our coverage. We try to address issues instantly during the games, but if not at that time, then at the end of the night. Instant problems might include Greg Gumbel not having the right statistics, or a certain affiliate not having the right game. Then Monday, Tuesday and Wednesday is spent preparing to go back on the air on Thursday night.

EAST REGION, YOU'RE CLEAR FOR TAKE-OFF

The way CBS Sports covers the tournament is extremely unique. There is no other sports broadcast where there are four games going on simultaneously. Our job, therefore, is like being an air traffic controller. We are trying to get viewers to the best games available. Games with home teams in local markets are going to be broadcast down to the sweet, or bitter, end. In other parts of the country, where there is no local team playing, we like to go to the best game at that particular time. If there is an upset in the making, we'll go to that game. Or, during half-time we like to show what else is happening around the country.

Coordinating things in the studio can get kind of hairy sometimes. Like an air traffic controller is coordinating four planes landing on one runway, we coordinate four regions on one network. Hopefully we can take everybody to game action somewhere in the country and provide them with a feeling of the intensity through highlights and scores, then take them out to live action of another game. We've pioneered and developed this system over the years.

We thought about how it would be great if, during halftime, people could see parts of the other games. It never had been like that before. In the past, all four regions tipped off at basically the same time, then hit halftime at about the same time. Our philosophy is to give people the most action possible. So, sitting at home, you might be watching game A, then at halftime be switched to games B, C and D. Then, when game A is over, ideally we take you to the finishes of games B, C and D, if they're all good. It gives the coverage a festival, or carnival, atmosphere, especially in the first and second rounds.

Trying to perfect this system has been difficult, but over the course of the tournament, instead of showing a couple of games, we have 63 games. We tell our producers going into the tournament that we will be asking them to do certain things that aren't done when just one game is on the air. We want the best possible coverage for the entire country. It's really a juggling act sometimes.

Final Four. Fast Facts

Steve Krafcisin is one of two players to play in two Final Fours for two different schools. Krafcisin played for North Carolina in 1977 and Iowa in 1980.

There have been situations in the past where we might have two buzzer-beater type games happening at the same time. So, we might literally switch viewers back and forth from game to game during time-outs. We hope to the people watching at home, that it looks easy and smooth. Behind the scenes it's complex.

In addition to being in charge of putting things together in the studio, such as the pregame, halftimes, and postgame show, as well as the *Road to the Final Four*, I also coordinate all the switching of games with Terry Ewert, Sean McManus and Mike Aresco. (McManus is the President of CBS Sports. Aresco is a Vice-President of Programming.)

Switching games is somewhat of a group decision. We watch different games in different areas of the building. Then, we ask Clark and our basketball experts if the game could turn out to be close. There might be eight minutes left to play in the game, but does team Y have a legitimate shot of making a comeback? Then, either Sean, Terry or Mike will make the final decision.

SIMPLY MADNESS

Basketball is terrific, but on the collegiate level it's even more exciting. Bringing out the emotion of the national tournament is something that we strive to do. Terry Ewert asks all of the producers and directors before the tournament starts to focus on the emotion of everyone involved. Also, these are college guys; they aren't pros. These are guys who are playing the game for the love of the sport. The college players are also younger, for the most part, so they offer their own true emotion. The cheerleaders, bands, and die-hard fans are all a part of the atmosphere. All of those factors play into the scene of the event.

Every year, as the stories continue, and the coverage and interest grows, it's a very easy event to get into. The basketball is pretty simple and, for the person at home, the tournament covers three weekends. People root for the school they attended, or the school nearby, or their state's school, which is obviously more diversified than the relatively small number of teams in a professional league. There are more opportunities to root for a college team.

With the way the tournament is set up, it seems like every person in the country has their own bracket, regardless if they're a college basketball fan or not. People don't necessarily have to follow college basketball all year to be interested in the tournament. Since the tournament is condensed into three different weekends, the person who is not a sports fan can fill out their office brackets and have a rooting interest in the teams like Gonzaga and Valpo.

And the fact that the tournament is one loss and you're out, makes it even more exciting. That's why we make sure we show everyone the big upsets. In a seven game series that underdog might be able to win one or two games, but won't necessarily advance in the tournament. Here, it's one shot. I love working the NCAA Tournament ... it's madness.

CHAPTER 23

Coach Wooden's Words of Wisdom

Former UCLA head coach John Wooden is considered by many to be the best college basketball coach of all time. Despite the fact that he is 13th overall in coaching victories (only one coach above Wooden has coached fewer years than his 29 – Jerry Tarkanian), there is no disputing his UCLA teams' domination of 10 NCAA titles in 12 seasons (second on that list is Adolph Rupp with four championships).

Wooden has been out of coaching since 1975, but he continues to teach basketball to anyone who will listen ... and who wouldn't listen to the wonder of Westwood? During interviews for the writing of *CBS Sports Presents: Stories from the Final Four,* Wooden offered the following nuggets of thought on various topics. Even though the comments were not appropriate for his stories of the 1964 and 1968 UCLA teams, they seem extremely timely for today's game.

ON THE FINAL FOUR ...

Some people say that with more teams playing in the tournament now, it is more difficult to win – I think more teams makes it easier. The first game of the tournament is when players get their tournament legs going. With more teams in the tournament, and the top teams opening with the No. 15 and No. 16 seeds, the better teams practically have a first-round bye. Also, with more teams in the tournament, there is more of a likelihood that a team could get in with 10 or more losses on the season. That is a lot of games to lose and still get in the tournament. Our 10 national championship teams only lost a total of 10 games. So the tournament has changed that way.

I've advocated very much, since they've gone to 64 teams, to just let all of the teams play in the tournament. Start it one week earlier, cut the season one week short because now they are playing too many games anyway, and let every single team in the tournament; then schools would get money for each game their team plays, instead of the tournament champion taking home $1.5 million. Obviously half of the field would be eliminated after the first round, but many of those eliminated teams need $60,000-$70,000, more than the winner needs $1.5 million.

I've advocated that all along. It wouldn't be difficult. There would still be complaints because of the way teams would be seeded, but we will always have unhappy teams.

ON UCLA'S DOMINATION ...

How many times had a team dominated the NCAA Tournament before our run? If it was easier back then with fewer teams in the tournament, then why hadn't it been done before us? I would say it is possible today for a team to dominate over a number of years, but it is not probable. There are things that people suggest make it more difficult now, such as players leaving school early. There are so many good players coming up now, though, that the good teams with a tradition are still going to get a lot of the good players. You don't see Kansas, North Carolina, Duke, UCLA and a number of the others ever lacking for material. They all have it. Comparing teams back in the 1960s and 1970s, there weren't as many good players.

We've all heard the statement, "It's more difficult to stay on top than it is to get there." I disagree with that 100 percent. We learn so much on the way to getting there, then once we're at the top, we're going to be up there where we can be a challenger. Getting there is tougher. Once you get up there, it's going to be much easier to stay in the running year after year. It's just awfully difficult to get there as today's programs are realizing.

ON GIVING 100% ...

There's no such thing as an over-achiever. I hear writers and broadcasters say, "He's an over-achiever." There's never been an over-achiever in anything. We're all under-achievers to different degrees; but we are all under-achievers, there's no question about that. I never wanted activity without achievement, either. I wanted achievement. I didn't want my team just running around wild. Instead, I wanted my teams to try and reach their maximum potential, which might have helped us achieve our goal.

ON RECRUITING ...

The one aspect of coaching that I didn't care for was recruiting, but there are other coaches that like it. I personally contacted very few recruits in my 27 years at UCLA. Most of our recruiting was done by one of my assistants. In most college basketball cases, it's the assistants that do most of the leg work on the recruiting. Then the head coach will be the determining factor in whether or not the student-athlete comes to that school.

I would never go recruiting a player like our coaches do now. I'm not saying this critically, I'm just saying that times have changed. Coaches in this era have been to Europe, Africa, and other faraway places. A great many of the coaches are doing that now. Some were doing it then, too, but not nearly to the extent that they do today.

The recruit, or someone for them, made the first contact with our program. I never initiated contact with a single prospect. Even Lew Alcindor's high school coach contacted me first. I never visited Lewis in any way to recruit him.

We never initiated contact with players, and I never had anyone initiate it for me. The contact had to come from the recruit. I'm not saying that no one from UCLA ever first called a player – they might have – but I didn't have them do it. I really wanted the player to have a desire to be at UCLA.

That's something of which I'm proud because I didn't want to talk players into coming. I thought we would have a much happier player if he really wanted to come play for us. If we talked him into coming and things didn't work out, then he would be down and would possibly affect others around him. I told every player, no matter who he was, that if he came to UCLA he'd be unhappy the first year, maybe a little more than that; then, if he stuck it out, he would be very pleased. That would be true of any college freshman. Being away from home for the first time can be quite an adjustment. That's why I think it's so terrible that freshmen are eligible to play varsity basketball. Going to college is a great social adjustment as well as academic, and players need a year to make the adjustment.

Look back at our record. I firmly believe in my own mind that if freshmen had been eligible in my day, we would have had another title. If Alcindor had been eligible as a freshman, we would have, but that's not known; it just feels that way. Still, I'm glad freshmen were not eligible.

ON THE STATE OF COLLEGE BASKETBALL ...

I have been a speaker at the McDonald's High School All American game every year since that started, mainly discussing academics, and how an education is the main reason for players going to college. A young player should not be focusing on a professional basketball career, regardless of how talented he might be.

Years ago there was a way to stop players from leaving school early, when pro teams couldn't draft them until the end of four years after graduating from high school. That rule was challenged and the courts did away with it. I know a lot of the pros wish there was still a rule like that. They feel it would be a better college game and a better pro game. Unfortunately, it can't be done legally, even though drafting players early has brought more problems.

ON COLLEGE BASKETBALL IN THE 21ST CENTURY ...

There should possibly be some concern about the collegiate game of basketball in terms of teamwork as we look ahead to the early part of the next century, because younger players are on a trend of playing too much like the professionals. The pros, who unquestionably have to play more for the fans, have developed quite a bit of showmanship. The showmanship brand of basketball comes down to the college players and even down to the interscholastic players. To me, it seems (although I could be completely wrong) that we don't see as much of the basic fundamentals.

There is tremendous individual athleticism, but not as fine of fundamental play as we have had in the past. Players have become better, but team play has gone the other way. That's natural. As the players improve individually, consciously or subconsciously, coaches will let them go on their own more, which hurts team play. The dunk and the 3-point shot are spectacular, and bring enormous reaction from the fans, but they have hurt team play overall. Where is the teamwork in a windmill dunk? Television, and its sensationalism, has had a lot to do with that showmanship and individualism. I'd like to see a more fundamental game. If I want to see showmanship, I'll go watch the Globetrotters play. If the players have become better and better, it stands to reason that so have the coaches, but great team play is a rarity.

The best pure basketball that people can experience today is among the better collegiate women's teams. They play below the rim and there isn't as much showmanship. I hope they can keep their play pure, but I am concerned that they will not.

On the men's side, officials also are letting things slide which has changed the game. For instance, they are permitting too much physical play in the game. There is a great inconsistency in calling moving screens, and dribblers are allowed to carry the ball more often without being called. Traveling is seldom called. If a player is going in for a dunk, he can nearly take as many steps as he wants. I've talked to officials about that who have said that the crowd loves it – particularly the pro officials with whom I have spoken.

Those are the things about the game that concern me. However, basketball is still a beautiful game, even with some of the showmanship. It is still the best spectator sport of all because it is played with a larger object that is easier to watch. A baseball and a hockey puck can be difficult to follow. The fans are closer to the action; and it's a game of action.

The college game will always be strong. Outside influences such as the CBA luring high school players should not have a long-term effect on college basketball. It will take a few players away who may have played in college, but the college game should not be hurt significantly by events like the CBA or by the players who do leave early for the NBA. Maybe the players leaving early, or going to other leagues instead of college, will bring about more parity among college teams. It may even bring back more fundamental basketball.

About the Editor

Matt Fulks, a native of Overland Park, Kan., started his media career while attending Lipscomb University in Nashville, Tenn. Since then, he has been involved in every form of media, including work with Nashville's NBC affiliate, WSMV-TV, and WAKM radio, covering high school, college, and professional sports.

Currently Matt is a weekly columnist for *Sportsnote.com*; as well as a regular contributor to the online magazine, *SchoolSports*. He is the author of *Behind the Stats: Tennessee's Coaching Legends* and *The Sportscaster's Dozen: Off the Air with Southeastern Legends*. Fulks also co-authored *Play by Play: 25 Years of Royals on Radio*, the auto-biography of Kansas City Royals broadcasters Denny Matthews and Fred White.

Matt resides in Atlanta with his wife, Libby, their daughter, Helen, and their Doberman retriever, Alex.